Give A Damn!®

Give A Damn!®

**INDIVIDUALLY WE MAKE A DIFFERENCE,
COLLECTIVELY WE CHANGE THE WORLD!**

FRANKIE:

Thank you for your support.

Mark S. Lewis

5/21/17

Mark S. Lewis

Registered in U.S. Patent and Trademark Office
Library of Congress Control Number: 2016907110
CreateSpace Independent Publishing Platform
North Charleston, South Carolina

This book is dedicated to all my friends who
have encouraged me to write this book especially:

my wife Elizabeth Lewis, my Dad, C. S. Lewis,
my twin sister, Kim Lewis James,
my father-in-law, Doug Connell,
Clayton White, Carl Gould, Christina Hildner,
Aaron Edge, Sunay Patel, Tony Romanos,
Thomas Brown, Mike Walker, AJ Levin,
and many more

**Above all, this book is
dedicated to my Mom,**

**Shirley B. Lewis
(April 9th, 1926 – November 19, 2012)**

She had a wonderful and loving heart!

Mom truly knew how to
GIVE A DAMN!

But more than anything she
SHARED HER LOVE!

Special Thanks to Amy Rose Pitonek
who provided countless hours of editing
and revisions. Amy was the final driving
force to complete this book after
many, many years.

Front Cover Illustrator: Jason Niebrugge

All inquiries, including bulk purchases
and discounts should be addressed to:

Mark S. Lewis
GIVE A DAMN! Enterprises LLC
6709 Avenue A
New Orleans, LA 70124
www.giveadamnbook.com
mlewis@giveadamnbook.com

Chapters

Foreward

I have no scientific proof to back any of my opinions, claims or statements in this book. I have done some market research but I am not a doctor or a psychologist (although my kids might think I need one ☺). The basis for my assertions is just common sense and basic reasoning, two traits that appear to be lacking in a lot of people these days. It's not that hard.

What I write is what I feel in my heart. It is what I have observed and experienced over several years and what I think is common sense. I am discouraged by the ongoing transition of today's society into selfishness, complacency, violence and irresponsibility. It all seems very simple to me. We need to start to **GIVE A DAMN** about other people and our world (and not just to those whom we are closest). People who **GIVE A DAMN** do the right thing and for the right reasons. They take responsibility for their actions and inactions, and they do it **ALL** of the time. It's not complicated, yet changing a mindset is the big challenge.

I have been formulating the ideas for this book over many years of observing the ways in which people interact with each other. Whenever I talk to others about the concepts in this book, they are usually very quick to agree with me. Few would argue against such values as responsibility, trustworthiness, and caring for others. However, while a majority of people will agree with me in theory, the majority of them don't actively **GIVE A DAMN**. In my opinion, there are two reasons for this: 1) they either don't *really* care, or more importantly, 2) they don't know how to. Many people are simply unaware of their own attitudes, actions (or lack thereof) and the effects of their behavior on others. They mean well, but fail to change their actual behavior, unless doing so will benefit them in some way. They don't realize how self-serving their actions really are, and I am not sure it's entirely their fault.

Our thoughts and feelings shape every aspect of our lives. No one can feel for you. It's not your family, your boss, bad luck, the economy, other people or anything else that makes you act a certain way, holds you back, or causes you angst. It is your own thoughts and feelings. These thoughts are shaped by everything that goes on around you (including what influences you) and they also determine your response to any situation. The goal of **GIVE A DAMN** is to help you develop a greater awareness of the thoughts that currently or eventually lead you to selfish and irresponsible behaviors. Many of these poisonous thoughts are so subtle that you are probably not even aware of them. However, as you become conscious of them you will then be able to behave in more generous and altruistic ways, especially toward others. This process takes time and effort, but I promise you it is worth it. It is worth it for our country and for the world. Once you are more aware of your thoughts and their influence on your actions, you will begin to truly know how to **GIVE A DAMN.**

I know change is tough. Learning how to **GIVE A DAMN** will be a big challenge but the world needs it badly. It's attainable, I know it. You will have challenges along the way, but you should never give up. My dream with **GIVE A DAMN** is to help change people's thinking process for the better, one person at a time. I want to make this world a better place for both present and future generations.

My hope for this book is that people will understand, develop and implement the themes I present; and that this will lead them to act in big and small ways to help others in every circumstance possible, regardless of convenience or personal benefit. My objective is to teach this world (and you, specifically) what it really means to **GIVE A DAMN**.

This book will help you towards that initiative. And guess what? I firmly believe that you will be happier and more successful than ever before, as long as that success is not your primary goal. Just do it and you will reap the benefits. In other words, you should **GIVE A DAMN** because it is the right thing to do, and it is what our world really needs. Read on and you will better understand why.

Throughout this book, I will give examples and make comments that may seem to be repetitive. I do this in a variety of ways and on purpose because of my desire to drive home important and key points. The more you read and hear something that you begin to believe in, the more likely it will become part of you and that is my ultimate goal. Please join me as this book starts the process of how and why you should **GIVE A DAMN!**

Before I dig further, let me make an important point. I have heard comments that the phrase **GIVE A DAMN** might come across as a harsh and possibly an offensive statement to some people. I refer to this statement many times throughout this book. My objective to drive home a point; and then I ask myself, "Would God or my Mom be offended by my title?" I am not swearing in the strictest sense. I think Mom would be okay with this slogan because I am hoping to help others, not swear like people do when they speak the word

"DAMN." I think God understands my words and He would support my message and intentions. I think you will agree as you read on.

However, you still might disagree with me so here is the solution: whenever you see the phrase, **GIVE A DAMN**, swap it out with **"SHARE YOUR LOVE,"** because this is *really* what it's all about.

CHAPTER 1

Why I Am FED Up and You Should Be Too!

Who doesn't think that we have become a more selfish and violent society? I certainly do. I would say that over the past 30 – 40 years we don't care as much for others as we used to, especially those we don't know. A big reason for this has been the advent of technology. Technology is decreasing face to face interaction to a greater extent than ever before. With advances in technology, we can do things faster, but this comes at a behavioral cost.

Many people expect the best, but they are only willing to put in a minimum of effort to get it. Some may call this efficiency, but there is a difference between efficiency and laziness! Sadly, in today's society, the mere mention of effort is taboo. And yet we want to be rewarded greatly for participating with little to no effort.

We have also become fixated on the idea of instant gratification. We want what we want when we want it (and that "when" is usually right away!). And if things don't go our way, it is not *our* fault, but the fault of someone else, or some circumstance, or the environment. The list is infinite! We are experts at blaming everyone and anything, but not ourselves. People just don't like to admit when they are wrong, although more often than not, they are.

People seem to place less value on serving others, being polite, taking responsibility, or showing respect. This attitude, combined with a lack of compassion for others, shows up in all sorts of places. We see it in people young and old, regardless of race, religion, occupation or persuasion. Let me offer a few examples below. These examples may seem negligible in the grand scheme of the world's problems. However, they are indicative of the toxic mindset that is rapidly becoming all too commonplace.

Several years ago, I went to a well-known fast food restaurant with my daughter, who was 10 years old at the time. The restaurant was rather empty, and we were the only ones in line. We noticed that an employee was having trouble with the cash register. She was so absorbed in her task that she didn't even notice us when we approached the counter. We waited patiently as she grew more and more agitated. The next word out of her mouth was, "SH**!" loud and clear. This was a supervisor, too! My daughter and I looked at each other in amazement, yet it didn't phase this woman one bit! She acted as if she was the only person in the room. Eventually, another supervisor came over to help and fixed the problem. Oh yeah, and then she took our order. The actions and language used by the first supervisor were totally inappropriate in the presence of any customer, but especially in front of a 10 year old child! Children are like sponges, they absorb the language, actions, and mannerisms of everyone around them, and usually can't distinguish which ones to discard as inappropriate. I was beside myself. How could anyone find such behavior acceptable? And without any apology for what she had done!

Another incident occurred during a visit to a grocery store. While trying to exit the store, I was held up by a long line of cars, all of which were waiting behind two young women who had stopped in the middle of the parking lot. One began to fish for something in her purse. As the line of cars grew, the first car in line lightly tapped on the horn. The two women began to casually and slowly move out of the roadway while one of them gave the car an obscene hand gesture. My first thought was, "Are you kidding me?" Neither of them had any concern for what they were doing or how it might affect others. I am sure they felt that they were doing nothing wrong, otherwise they would not have reacted the way they did. It didn't bother them one bit that they were holding up traffic, or even that they were in harm's way. Instead of blocking the road, why couldn't they have entered the store and then dealt with the purse? Is this not just common sense?

It's entirely possible that the people mentioned in these examples truly didn't know what they were doing. Maybe the supervisor at the register had never been taught which language was appropriate to use around children, or that servicing customers takes priority over anything. Maybe her parents used that word around her all the time. Perhaps those two women in the parking lot were so caught up in what they were doing that they didn't even notice the line of cars that was forming behind them. Should everyone be given the benefit of the doubt, even those who appear to simply not **GIVE A DAMN**? I am not sure, but I don't think so. Over the past 20 – 30 years, parents have become less concerned with teaching their children values such as respect, responsibility, and common courtesy. By the time these children are adults or even 12 or 13 years old, their give or don't **GIVE A DAMN** mentality is probably already formed. You can't fault someone who doesn't know. You can only try to teach them a better way. Maybe this book will help.

The statement, "That's not my job" is becoming all too common these days and is a sure indication of someone who has an "all about me" attitude. People who make this statement surely do not **GIVE A DAMN** about helping anyone else, unless it might serve their best interests. For instance, let's say you are at work and have a really important project to get out. It's 3:00 PM on Tuesday and you have two hours to get it done. You know you need help, so you ask your associate (we will call him Pete) to make copies so you can meet your fast approaching deadline. Upon hearing your request, Pete replies, "Sorry, that's just not my job." You think, "Really?" and are quick to add, "Pete, I really need to get this done. I will give you 50 bucks if you help me." Without hesitation, Pete says, "Sure!"

So now Pete offers his help because it has a material benefit for him, which took precedence over you. There seems to be a growing trend that people are less likely to do good things for others simply because it is the right thing to do. Rather, they need some kind of reward or accolade (like money) to motivate them. It is a sad and disturbing tendency which has become more prevalent every day.

The picture below depicts a classic example of a "Not my Job!" attitude. It was not the job of the street painters to remove the dead animal in the road so they simply painted over it. Pretty classic but at the same time, pretty sad.

My next example is about greed and underhanded tactics. It shows that people who don't **GIVE A DAMN** are as common in the business world as anywhere else. As a property owner in a small town, I was contacted several years ago by a small company who asked me to consider placing a billboard on my property. My property was one of the few left outside the city limits that could have a billboard. I received their proposal and decided to contact a large publicly traded company for a similar proposal. I told them about my property and they gave me an offer which was not nearly as attractive. Therefore, I decided to contract with the smaller company and told the publicly traded company about my decision. Unbeknownst to me, the larger company immediately went to the property owner next door and had them sign a billboard lease, which required the filing of a permit with the local government. Since they acted so quickly, I could no longer do business with the smaller company due to a law requiring a 500-foot variance between billboards. I was out. They knew the circumstances behind their actions and played dumb when I called them about it. No law was broken, except for the law of right and wrong. Their selfish approach to doing business caused me to lose revenue that I would have generated by having the billboard on my property. It was also to the detriment of the smaller company. I wrote a letter to the company explaining the circumstance but nothing came of it. Here's the kicker: as of today, the larger company never did put a billboard on the adjacent property.

My next and final example really hurts. In 2008, a video began circulating on the Internet. It was a surveillance camera tape of an old man crossing the street one July evening in Hartford, Connecticut. Nothing unusual, until the man was suddenly struck by a car (1). The vehicle was only traveling about 20 miles an hour but the impact was significant, causing the man to flip over and land on his head in the middle of the street. The driver did not stop, and as the man lay there injured, no one came to help. Car after car swerved around him and went on their way. This went on for a whole minute (although while watching the video it felt like hours) before someone eventually came to his aid. Stop and look at your watch and see how long a minute can be! You cannot imagine how many cars went past him without stopping to help.

Now, if you were driving your car past this man and noticed it was your grandfather, what would you do? Would you come to his aid immediately? **DAMN** right you would. The fact that no one helped for over a minute was mind boggling to me. Maybe people were scared by what they saw or feared getting involved because they might be blamed if something went wrong. Who knows? But any excuse not to help this man is a lousy one. There had to be at least twenty people who were aware of the incident and not one of them bothered to help. This is a classic example of people who just did not **GIVE A DAMN**. Oh, by the way, the old man who was hit? He died.

Now get this. I came across another video that showed a dog hit by a car. The dog was lying in the middle of a major highway, yet was still alive. As the video played, another dog dodged on-coming traffic to help the injured dog, while not one person stopped to help. The dog ran over to the injured dog, grabbed him with his mouth, and carried him out of harm's way, nearly getting hit several times. Guess what? The dog lived.

What a contrast, huh? Human versus dog and the dog wins. The dog saved one of its own kind because he knew how to **GIVE A DAMN**. Is that possible? Dogs aren't supposed to have brains like we do, but clearly we could learn a thing or two from them. Aren't they always happy to see you? Don't they always want to please you? Maybe the dog instinctively knew he was doing the right thing, no matter the personal risk involved in saving another. Then again maybe the dog knew that whatever happened he could not get sued!! We humans are supposedly smarter than dogs. Maybe we need to incorporate this same kind of doggie attitude into our own behavior. Maybe we should have this kind of mentality: "Let me be the person my dog thinks I am." Read it again. "Let me be the person my dog thinks I am."

So now you know why I am fed up. I see instances every day in which people just don't **GIVE A DAMN**, and they can always find some form of justification for not doing so. I am simply fed up with the continuous inconsiderate don't **GIVE A DAMN** attitudes and actions like those listed above. Each and every one of these cases forms another unstable building block in the self-serving structure of our society; feeding itself like a cancer. I am fed up with people being too busy, greedy and selfish to do the right thing, or to take responsibility for their actions. There seems to be no more consequences for our deeds or actions, just excuses and bailouts. It always seems to be someone else's fault. Society's continued self-serving attitude certainly cannot lead to anything good in the future; and it certainly hasn't in the past. This cancerous pattern needs to be broken and a **GIVE A DAMN** attitude will cure it. There are too many things going on in the world that breed a don't **GIVE A DAMN** attitude. We need to change our mindset and *change it now* because:

**Individually we make a difference,
collectively we change the world**!

(1) https://www.youtube.com/watch?v=xjrqkT13dGo

CHAPTER 2

How Did We Get Where We Are Today?

What happened to our society of 50 years ago? In the past we seemed to care more about others than we do today. Good deeds and a strong work ethic were highly valued. Cheating, lying, laziness, bad language and greed were frowned upon, whereas now these behaviors and characteristics are tolerated, even among our leaders. Many individuals get away with them because they have no fear of repercussions if they are caught. In fact, these traits are almost admired! We see this type of behavior all over TV, radio and social media outlets; and this behavior seems encouraged because it's perceived as "funny" or "clever." We laugh these things off instead of being horrified, excusing them with phrases such as, "You've got to hand it to him… he got away with it," or "It's not real, it's only TV." It's not funny because it's like a cancer, it breeds upon itself. Incomprehensible actions that show up in the media are seeping their way into engulfing our society.

We no longer have the many positive role models that once taught us how to **GIVE A DAMN**. Andy Griffith and the Brady Bunch have been replaced with scantily-dressed pop stars, trashy televised "reality shows" and many over-paid athletes who care only for themselves and are often above reproach. We all know there are exceptions to everything but these elements seem to be more and more common-place than ever before.

Songs today now have more swear words than ever before. Fifty years ago we would not have tolerated such language. The children growing up today are learning from various outlets that such behavior is okay and that it often pays to be vulgar, dishonest, selfish and sneaky because it is supposedly "cool" and/or "funny."

Of course, there are artists and other people who do their best to carry themselves well and deliver a positive message, but they are few and far between. In addition, they often do not receive the same amount of advertising money or media coverage that less scrupulous stars do because it won't bring in ratings, thus hindering their success. Scandalous behavior attracts more attention, which is exactly what media moguls want: sensationalism……. which = ratings!

In my unscientific research and observations, I think there are nine primary elements that explain how we got to our current state. I am sure there are others but I firmly believe these elements (that unknowingly work together) have had the most profound effect on the degradation of our society. The combination of these elements is the feeding mechanism for most of the others, and they can be divided into what I believe are these institutional and societal categories:

1. Government
2. Special Interest Groups
3. The Legal System
4. Education
5. Religion
6. Family Values
7. Wealth
8. Technology
9. Media

People who don't **GIVE A DAMN** are everywhere. At first, I thought it was just in my city. It is not just a geographical or a big city attitude; it is prevalent across our nation and the world. This gets down to the very core of our society. Changing attitudes about what is acceptable has caused the world to become way too self-centered. People rarely admit when they make a mistake (because we have so many choices to make in every situation) and it always seems to be the fault of some outside force that influences their actions. We always have an excuse but rarely take responsibility. Why is it that society generally does not **GIVE A DAMN**?

There are three primary reasons:

1) We have become a self-centered and greedy culture;
2) There is no foundation for how to **GIVE A DAMN** because it is not taught in our schools or at home and,
3) Society and the government breed an entitlement philosophy rather than one of responsibility.

The next two chapters will go over in detail each of the nine elements within our institutions and society that are contributing factors into what is a don't **GIVE A DAMN** attitude or mentality. After identifying these problems, I will go on to offer solutions in the final chapters of this book. Read on to find out why our lack of a **GIVE A DAMN** attitude is killing society and what we can do as individuals (working together) to fix it. Again,

**Individually we make a difference,
collectively we change the world!**

CHAPTER 3

Institutional Effects on Society - It's a Problem

Although our legal and governing institutions have had a long and successful history, they have veered off their path in terms of what they are supposed to do for society. Instead of being pillars of society, many government and non-government institutions have begun to encourage greed, censorship, and the lack of responsibility among citizens. In many cases this has been going on for years! As a result, changes are vastly needed. This chapter will outline the four domains in which change is needed the most: government, Special Interest Groups, the legal system, and our education system.

Government

For the most part, our current state of government both at the state and federal level breeds entitlement. Who would argue this except the people getting the entitlement? I know it's a pretty bold statement but I think it's true. Some might say, "Without the government we could not survive. Our government cares about everyone. Look at all they've done for us!" I agree, but generally, today's government breeds a self-centered society that encourages a, "What can the government do for me?" mentality.

As a result of government policies, society has lost its self-reliance, confidence and willingness to take on accountability. People have been conditioned to think more about what they can get out of a situation versus what they can put into it. It is written in the Bible (Luke 6:38), "Give and it will be given to you," meaning that the more we put into something the more we'll get out of it. Yet at the same time, (based on our giving), we should not *expect* to get anything in return for this giving. That's where people get it wrong. In reality, we *will always get* something in return! The problem is that people's thought process is often in reverse of what it should be because of their, "what's in it for me?" attitude.

Does the government teach responsibility or even exhibit responsibility in its own actions? Because of the way society has transitioned into a "me" centered culture and the ways that government has perpetuated this culture through ineffective welfare or other entitlement programs, a mechanism has been put in place for people to believe that they are owed something for merely existing. Lou Holtz, former college football coach (and a good one!) said it best:

"When we were growing up we had duties and responsibilities, now people feel like they have rights and privileges."

A lot of people think that since they pay taxes, they have the right to get a portion of that money back in some fashion. I'm not talking in terms of a tax refund, effective public education, or a well-maintained infrastructure. I'm talking about a sense of entitlement that spans across every income bracket, from the destitute to the very rich. Whether it's about people refusing to work over 20 hours a week in order to maintain welfare benefits, or massive subsidies for commercial farmers who are already making over $200,000 a year (1), the government channels its money into handouts rather than incentives. When government breeds this kind of entitlement, the population starts to *expect* that it will swoop in and take care of all their problems. Guess what? That's not government's job. Their job is to protect us, keep us safe and provide the infrastructure to help us succeed, not to hand out "entitlement" checks because of who you are, what happened to you or what you have paid into the system.

During the recovery process for Hurricane Katrina (2005), I saw a news report featuring a lady in public housing who had been displaced by the storm. She stated on TV, "The government owes me a place to stay, a place to live, based on what happened." She is basically saying that she had nothing to do with the flooding caused by Hurricane Katrina. What? Excuse me, but since when has it been written that the government is responsible for putting shelter over your head? Isn't that *your* responsibility? Then again, how can you blame her for making this statement? In some twisted way, she's right. For years the government has subsidized public housing and has done little to successfully help these people sustain life for themselves. They continue to stay in public housing because they don't know any other way. They can't take responsibility if they've never been taught the concept.

To solve this, we need to start giving people the reins to shape their own lives, allowing them to reap the benefits or suffer the consequences according to the decisions they make. We need to give them all the tools they need to have a good start in life, and then let them take control from there. But there needs to be an end point or finish line to government help. That is not happening today.

As I have stated before, there are always exceptions to every rule and I am in *no way* suggesting we turn our backs on people. The issue is not one of helping those who are truly in need, the issue is when the government feels like they have to do something to help people, *without emphasizing responsibility.* There is a difference between helping them and holding their hands. The government owes me nothing other than to keep me safe and to make sure I have the infra-structure in place to conduct my business and personal affairs. Isn't that why we pay taxes?

During the aftermath of Hurricane Katrina, there were a lot of people that did not have insurance on their homes (either by choice or because they just couldn't afford it). Many of them had homes that were either damaged or destroyed by the hurricane. The federal government then implemented the "Road Home" program (2), which offered rebuilding *grants* of up to $150,000 dollars for those whose homes were damaged. It also offered grants of up to $30,000 dollars for those who wished to elevate their homes as protection against future storms. The people who paid insurance for many years also got the benefit of a government bailout like the uninsured; yet it was often not nearly as much since FEMA does not duplicate money received from insurance companies. However, those whose insurance companies fought against paying them in full for damages sustained, did get paid whatever was deemed necessary to finish repairs. In one sense, you could that say everyone was treated equally. Both the insured and the uninsured received money from the federal government. The difference is that the insured had already paid years of premiums to protect their property while the uninsured had not.

So the common statement from the uninsured was that it wasn't their fault that Hurricane Katrina hit and the levies broke, or the levies were not built properly. I agree. But it was their choice not to get insurance. Why should the government offer bail out for any of these people? Shouldn't they suffer the con-sequences of their decisions? I am all about helping people but when decisions are made and it doesn't go your way, shouldn't you accept the consequences of that decision? Some might say that I have no compassion. Of course I do, but even when the consequences of your decisions aren't in your favor, you're still liable for them! Should someone else pay for *your* mistake? I don't think so. Not only that, but between $6 million to $1.4 billion dollars (quite a gap) of that relief money was found to be given away in error or misused (3)! According to a report by the Government Accountability Office, some of that "relief" money was used for such "so called" necessities as alcoholic beverages, tattoos, and a week-long vacation at a resort in the Dominican Republic. Our government seems to want to give something away for nothing. The only person who should take care of you is *you*, not the government.

I really do believe that our government wants to take care of people but not necessarily for the right reasons. First of all, if the government's intention was to truly get people on their feet, they would educate and assist people in taking more responsibility for their lives. Second, political decisions are often made based on how many votes a politician can possibly get, not because it is the right thing to do. The more the government provides, the more people will expect. This is what perpetuates the process of entitlement. So, here is a comprehensive list of everything you're entitled to and what the world owes you:

Nothing!

(1) https://www.washingtonpost.com/news/wonk/
    wp/2015/02/12/the-bachelor-billionaires-and-the-prob-
    lem-with-farm-subsidies-for-the-rich/, February 12, 2015. By
    Danielle Paquette
(2) https://www.road2la.org/. Road Home Program. US
    Department of Housing and Urban Development.
(3) http://www.gao.gov/new.items/d1017.pdf. January 2010.
    US Government Accountability Office.

Special Interest Groups

Our founding fathers worked together for the betterment of society; a society comprised of individuals and groups who would be *free to act* and *worship* as they pleased and speak their minds (obviously within limits). Today, our society is transitioning into people speaking and working solely towards their own interests. This causes them to judge (and even condemn) anyone who dares to think differently, because they view any difference in viewpoint as a threat to their own interests.

We all know that Special Interest Groups (SIGs) play a big role in both politics and business. Some are mass based like the AARP (formerly the American Association of Retired Persons) and the NRA (National Rifle Association), while business SIGs include the Chambers of Commerce, the AMA (American Marketing Association) and many others. There are probably hundreds if not thousands of them in each category. Yet, do we truly understand the extent to which SIGs shape our public or business policies, let alone our individual lives? Probably not.

Special Interest Groups were originally designed to assist marginalized groups of our population who were not given a voice or permitted equal rights. Without someone speaking up for minority groups, women might not have been granted the right to vote, and we might still have racially segregated schools. These Special Interest Groups are important, as are many others. However, SIGs now have become so prevalent and powerful in our political system, that sometimes the needs and interests of a few individuals outweigh the needs and interests of the majority of citizens to the point that the entire system is paralyzed, or at least dysfunctional.

Politicians often try to cater to the needs of Special Interest Groups (for votes and money) instead of the needs of the majority. Even if a law is good for 80% of the population, there seems to be some Special Interest Group influence that satisfies the minority rather than the majority. If a SIG were to **GIVE A DAMN**, then in most cases the majority would rule. Just like when a politician runs for office and wins with 50.01% of the vote, the majority rules. Yet the other losing 49.99% don't complain because *they have* to accept it. Unless the difference is only a couple of votes in an election, they accept the loss. Maybe the public should vote for everything?

There have been many studies done on the power that Special Interest Groups have over public policy. One particularly well known study is that of Gilens and Page, published in 2014. They demonstrated how economic elites and SIGs have a much greater sway over policy than the average citizen (1). This certainly makes sense because individually we can make a difference, but collectively (and with money) we have huge influence. The preferences of economic elites are often in line with you and me (the average citizen), and it leads to what is known as coincidental representation: the wishes of the average citizen are fulfilled without them having a direct influence on the process. Here's where it goes wrong. The Gilens study showed that the preferences of mass based Interest Groups are rarely in line with that of the public. The study further showed that the preferences of business oriented Interest Groups actually has a *negative correlation* with the preferences of both median income and affluent citizens! Even more disturbing is that business based Interest Groups currently make up about 84% of groups who lobby at the federal level (2)! Do you think that these people have the money to lobby for what they want? Absolutely. Do you think that the politicians listen because there is lots of money (and votes) involved? Absolutely. Do you think these SIGs do the right thing for the majority versus the minority? I am not so sure, but I suspect there is certainly a push-pull mechanism going on. In actuality, if these interest groups made a **GIVE A DAMN** decision, they would get the *right* answer every time. More on this later.

The SIG debacle is even more disturbing after the 2010 Supreme Court decision in the case of Citizen's United vs. the Federal Election Commission (FEC). It further amplified our country's Interest Group problem to unprecedented levels because their decision legalized *unlimited independent expenditures by unions and corporations* in favor of a candidate or party. In summary, the Court decided that defining corruption as *anything other* than an exchange of money to an office or potential office holder (politician) in return for a favor was a violation of the First Amendment. So they argued that as long as unions, corporations or anyone else was only contributing money to *support or oppose a political campaign,* (and therefore not directly involved with the office holder), campaign finance restrictions did not apply. Seriously? So the Supreme Court opened the door for a massive injection of money into subsequent political campaigns without retribution in any way. This gave anyone with enough money (and inclination) the ability to form so-called super PACs (political advocacy organizations) with massive budgets that may accept unlimited amounts of money from individuals, groups, or business, as long as they refrain from being directly involved with a candidate. Although they are limited from *supposedly* colluding directly with politicians, the super PAC's can spend an unlimited amount of money in support of one particular person without violating campaign laws. How does this pass the common sense test? It doesn't. And of course, many Special Interest Groups were in favor of this ruling (such as the Heritage Foundation and ACLU) because they can raise as much money as they want. What politician wouldn't want to be on one of these organizations good side?

The Citizen's United decision opened up a big can of worms because it set the precedent for rulings that have further undermined campaign finance law. Noting just a few more here:

1. **McCutcheon vs. the FEC** – This case struck down limits on aggregate campaign donations.
2. **SpeechNOW.org vs. the FEC** – This case legalized unlimited independent campaign expenditures by individuals.
3. **Western Tradition Partnership, Inc. vs. Montana** – And this case dealt a blow to an individual state's right to limit corporate campaign contributions.

Those in favor of these and many other decisions argue that money does not necessarily *guarantee* a win for a certain candidate (probably true); nor does spending in favor of a campaign influence a candidate's behavior once elected (probably not true). Let's use some common sense here, as I always like to look at extremes when trying to figure something out. For instance, if I had no money and wanted to run for office, would I have a snowball's chance of winning? No way. Now let's say my campaign had been bolstered by a billion dollars in donations, would I have a better chance of winning? Of course I would. Would I be indebted to those who provided me with a billion dollars to win a campaign? Why wouldn't I be? A **GIVE A DAMN** person would be very thankful for such support and want to return the favor in a rightful way. The problem is that the return of favors may be, and sometimes are, done for the wrong reasons.

For instance, if I were running for office and someone (or the masses) donated zillions of dollars to my campaign, I would make it very clear that any decision I made would be based on what is right for the majority, not because someone gave me the most money in order to get a political favor or votes for a second term (that's why I would only run for one term). I know it's not that simple, but its common sense and the right thing to do. Plus it's probably why I would never get elected anyway. Who would want to support my campaign (unless they were a true **GIVE A DAMN** person or organization) if I did not support what they wanted when I knew it was wrong?

The point is that if a politician's campaign has been aided with millions of dollars in advertising, demonstrations, and political pamphlets funded by a certain group, it is natural for the candidate to feel indebted to the group. Therefore, what the group *says* or better yet, "*implies*" to the politician can heavily influence his decision. And that decision is not necessarily based on choosing right from wrong when it comes to the best interest of the majority. Therefore the SIG wins. Plus, if a group finds a candidate that already supports their interests, why wouldn't they pour massive amounts of money into getting him elected? And that is certainly not a bad thing *if, and only if,* it supports the majority. Direct individual contributions to a candidate are still limited, so no one can write a million dollar check and mail it to their candidate of choice. But the Supreme Court gave corporations, unions, and Special Interest Groups the ability to collect and spend as much money as they see fit to "*independently*" advocate for a candidate. It's just not right and doesn't make sense. In the Supreme Court decision regarding Citizen's United and the many other cases that followed, the trend has gone towards allowing an unlimited amount of money into politics. Simple common sense says this is not a good thing because it opens the door for too many questionable decisions to be made (another great reason why I favor term limits). Now here is the next interesting question: If a SIG knew that a **GIVE A DAMN** politician would *always* make the right decision and it might go against them, would they still pour money into getting him elected? What do you think?

Besides money, influencing the decisions of politicians isn't the only area in which Special Interest Groups hold power. They also use litigation when necessary. This is not always a bad thing as it can sometimes be the only way for a disadvantaged group to gain their rights. A prime example of this is when the NAACP used litigation to fight for the desegregation of schools in the Brown vs. the Board of Education case (3). However, there seems to be an alarming trend that is shifting towards groups who not only argue their cause through a well-funded army of lawyers and experts, but also make massive donations towards electing judicial candidates that they deem favorable to their cause. In the post Citizen's United era, this has only gotten worse. In the 2013-2014 judicial election cycle, contributions from SIGs increased to a record 29% of total spending (4)! Twenty-one out of the 23 contested seats were won by the candidate who received the most money (4). Pretty good odds but the question begs, is this really how we want to decide our judiciary?

We are also seeing many ideological interest groups using their money and power to file lawsuits that force others to adhere to their particular belief system. A prime example that comes to mind is when the ACLU (in June 2007) supported an attack of a historical picture of Jesus hanging in a Slidell, LA courtroom. The ACLU argued that there needs to be a separation of church and state. This same picture had been hanging up in the courthouse for years and now, all of a sudden, it becomes a problem? What was the ACLU's motive? One person complains because it "offends them" and now it needs to come down? It's almost like this person thinks that the picture was directed at them. So don't look at it. If I see a picture that is offensive to me (and it really does not matter what it is) should I get an organization to file suit on my behalf to take it down? No. But there is a very easy solution to this issue and many issues like this: *Take a vote on it.* Let the citizens of Slidell vote on whether they want to keep the picture or not! And the majority wins. Seems really simple to me and passes the common sense test.

There is also evidence that Interest Group policies lead to a stagnant economy. Mancur Olson first argued this in 1982, stating that Special Interest Groups are costly to the economy, since their incomplete representation of society as a whole combined with the sway they exert over policy decisions leads to an inefficient allocation of resources. Instead of producing new wealth, their *lobbying* efforts are usually geared towards the redistribution of what already exists (5). Olson also stated that SIGs have the tendency to create barriers to market entry that impede innovation and new methods of production. In general, the more Interest Groups you add to a society, the less flexible and innovative it becomes. In some cases, the economic consequences of catering to Interest Groups can be disastrous. For instance, the expansive import duties of the Smoot Hawley Tariff of 1930 were heavily lobbied for by agricultural and industrial interest groups. Their success caused other countries to impose their own tariffs in retaliation, sharply decreasing American exports, and thus many jobs were lost. This hike in unemployment ended up being one of the contributing factors to the Great Depression.

A more recent study (6) of the economic effects of Interest Groups across 84 countries further confirmed the negative effect of SIGs on society. This study put Olson's theories to the test, and found that they still hold true today: Interest Groups were again found to have a negative effect on an economy's Gross Domestic Product, capital stock, and productivity growth. To be exact, they calculated that in the Organization of Economic Cooperation and Development (OECD) countries, each 1% increase in Interest Groups lowered the growth of a country between one half and three fourths of a percentage point (eye opening and quite startling!). This may not seem like a lot, but when you think about the vast number of Interest Groups in our country, it certainly adds up!

I am not saying that all Special Interest Groups are bad because they are not. The problem is that the good ones **GIVE A DAMN**, and many others don't. I am not about to identify who they are because I honestly don't know. But if each SIG had a **GIVE A DAMN** attitude, then they could contribute to the economy instead of taking away from it. Serving the majority and doing right from wrong is what it should be all about, and using common sense would be quite helpful as well.

So where do we start? A return to a democracy in which laws are made for and decided by the *people* instead of allowing politicians to succumb to the pressure of Special Interest Groups when deciding policy would be a great beginning. Let the people decide, but can we get the politicians to take this directive? The politician mindset has to change to a **GIVE A DAMN** attitude that gives the people a much greater voice in deciding policy for themselves; no matter what the issue (I'll have more recommendations on this later). When an issue comes up, let the vote of the citizens decide, not the politicians. If over 50% of the population supports a law or decision, politicians should not have the right to decide against it based upon the fear of negative publicity, capital flight or other negative consequences that might come from a certain group.

I think that most would agree that many politicians make decisions for two reasons: to get votes that will enable them to stay in office, and/or to secure future funding. They are not as concerned about what it is in the best interests of the mass (although they will tell you differently), but rather what is in the best interests of those with money and influence, and how it might directly affect them. It would take a unique politician to **GIVE A DAMN** for the whole, rather than a piece. Do you know anyone like this? Adding fuel to this directive was a poll taken by the New York Times/CBS in 2015, which revealed that 84% of respondents said there was too much money involved in politics (7). I agree because it influences people to make the wrong decisions and for the wrong reasons. Money is power and most of the money that is raised for politicians comes from Special Interest Groups. There is no argument in that!

However, there is a catch. It's true that many Special Interest Groups distort our political system in an unhealthy way, but the majority isn't always right either. Sometimes people make decisions irrationally, or based off of incorrect information. What comes to mind is Ibsen's famous play, "A Public Enemy." In this play, the majority of the townspeople override a doctor's report that a hot spring resort in their town was contaminated, thus incorrectly (and for the wrong reason) deciding to keep and promote a severe public health hazard. They never did ask the question: What's the right thing to do? They did not **GIVE A DAMN** because they made a self-serving decision to the detriment of others, but they did it in support of themselves. The consequence of doing the right thing was going to be quite painful to their community, so they justified making the wrong decision because it was right for them. The majority can become extremely destructive when it is driven by self-serving motives. This is why we need to shape our society into a **GIVE A DAMN** society that is responsible enough to serve the greater good.

Many academics would argue that it could be very dangerous to allow the average citizen to have a large influence (or vote) over foreign policy because, in all fairness, they just do not have the expertise to do so. They make the simple point that only half of Americans know where Syria is located on a map! So they ask the question, do we really want the other half weighing in on the Middle East policy decisions? I agree, we should allow the experts to make decisions on foreign policy but only if they know how to **GIVE A DAMN**. The issues here are a whole lot more dynamic because in a lot of cases you are dealing with unreasonable self-centered people, and that creates a whole new dynamic when making **GIVE A DAMN** choices on foreign policy. But the **GIVE A DAMN** premise should be the over-riding factor, and *only* if it protects our freedom and security. The problem is that some business oriented Special Interest Groups have way too much sway when it comes to US foreign policy and the experts are not much, if at all involved (8). This can be very dangerous because in many cases these groups have a monetary interest in getting their way, and also do not necessarily have the knowledge or desire to do what is truly best for the people. Foreign policy becomes even more delicate and demanding to the **GIVE A DAMN** person.

The question is this: Can we fix these problems to create a more informed public and a more democratic society? Only if we *all* (or a vast majority) were to have a **GIVE A DAMN** attitude and mind-set. Impossible? I don't think so. Practical? Yes. *But we have to start somewhere!*

The best and most effective way to start is to push for a better educated society across all levels, and to start at an early age. It will take many, many years to change a mindset of a society but some-one has to start the process. When I say education, I mean two levels: scholastic and character, which I will delve into in greater detail later.

We need to teach the critical thinking skills to make the right choices over and over again and in every situation. Complete trans-parency, proper manners and communication protocols should be encouraged in all of our institutions and political establishments; this same honesty and transparency in the media is paramount as well (more on this later too!). How can people truly vote if they don't re-ally know the undistorted facts behind an issue?

I am not professing this to be easy. It will require a major overhaul of our current political system and the whole method of how each of us thinks, especially Special Interest Groups. Someone needs to step up and lead this charge (and change) because we just can't just sit around and wait for it to happen. Change is needed for Special Interest Groups to think differently and to help in this process. **GIVE A DAMN** politicians, lawmakers and *everyone else* needs to do what we can to instill an attitude and action of doing right from wrong.

To quote astrophysicist Neil Degrasse Tyson: "I dream of a world where the truth is what shapes people's politics, rather than politics shaping what people think is true." All it would take is for everyone to **GIVE A DAMN**.

(1) Gilens, Martin and Page, Benjamin. 2014. *Testing Theories of American Politics: Elites, Interest Groups, and Average Citizens.* Perspectives on Politics 12 (3). 564-576.

(2) de Figueiredo, John M and Kelleher Richter, Brian. 2014. *Advancing the Empirical Research on Lobbying.* Annual Review of Political Science 17. 163-185.

(3) "Case: Landmark: Brown vs Board of Education" NAACP Legal Defense and Education Fund, Inc. Web. 20 January 2016.

(4) Greytak, Scott, et al. 2015. *Bankrolling the Bench: The New Politics of Judicial Elections 2013-14.* Brennan Center for Justice.

(5) Olson, Mancur. 1982. *The rise and decline of nations: the political economy of economic growth, stagflation, and social rigidities.* New Haven: Yale.

(6) Coates, Dennis, Heckelman, Jac C., and Wilson, Bonnie. 2010. *Special Interest Groups and Growth.* Public Choice 147. 496-457.

(7) Confessore, Nicholas and Thee-Brenan, Megan. "Poll Shows Americans Favor an Overhaul of Campaign Finance." New York Times. 2 June 2015. Web.

(8) Jacobs, Lawrence and Page, Benjamin. 2005. *Who Influences Foreign Policy?* American Political Science Review. 99 (1). 107-121.

The Legal System

Personally, I think the legal system is also to blame for people who don't **GIVE A DAMN**. We have become such a litigious society, which has caused us to become more focused on what we can gain monetarily from a situation as opposed to what is actually right or wrong. People can get sued for helping others even if their intention is good. The legal system has awarded people millions of dollars for the most frivolous things, which encourages even more law suits. It seems that you cannot make a mistake in this world today without the potential threat of being sued (especially if you can sue someone who you think has loads of money), and that my friend is one reason why a lot of people don't **GIVE A DAMN**.

There are a lot of people looking for any reason to sue someone, waiting for that perfect angle to hit the home run. Why doesn't someone just sue everybody for everything that might be bad for them? We all know that a doughnut is not as healthy for us as an apple. For example, a guy named Jack developed a love for doughnuts. This love caused him to eat multiple doughnuts every day for years, and thanks to a high metabolism, he was never overweight. After many years of gorging on doughnuts, Jack had a heart attack and died at an early age. An autopsy showed Jack's clogged arteries were the cause of his death, yet there was no heart disease in Jack's family. One of Jack's friends publicly stated that he had an addiction to doughnuts for years. Jack's family doctor stated that this was the likely cause for his clogged arteries. Upon hearing this, one of Jack's family members decided to sue the local doughnut shop for their role in contributing to the Jack's death. Of course this example is fictional, but if it really did occur, would it surprise you? There are literally hundreds of similar "real and crazy" incidents like this every year that are litigious. Here is my point: How in the world can you blame a company for the choices a person makes (unless there is indisputable evidence otherwise)? Jack died because he made the conscious decision to eat hundreds of thousands of doughnuts. He had to have known this wasn't a healthy choice. So a person likes to blame someone else or some event that happened to him (looking outside) rather than looking at how his actions (or lack thereof) might have contributed to his situation (looking inside).

Frivolous lawsuits send a message to millions of other people and their attorneys: "If anything happens to you, you can sue because it might be their fault. And guess what? You never know what a jury might think and you might hit a big payday, so let's go for it!" One thing has led to another and now you see all kinds of attorneys making commercials stating, "You could be entitled to a large cash award!" You know why I don't like lawyers who take cases like this? Because most don't **GIVE A DAMN** about what is right and what is wrong. They take the chance because of what stupid juries have awarded in the past on frivolous lawsuits. And I have to believe, that in their guts, they know what is right and what is not. They don't seem to care about the massive amounts of tax payer dollars that are wasted on frivolous lawsuits, either. They only care about that potential winning and making the big bucks. It is a crying shame and the judicial system is equally at fault for letting this problem become so widespread. Sure, some cases are legitimate but many are not.

One day, I came upon a bus that had been involved in a minor accident. A lot of people were coming off the bus complaining about injured necks and/or backs. When these people were told that there was a camera on the bus that captured the accident, they miraculously healed from their wounds. They were obviously looking for that big payday and lying was their ticket. It's just so sad that people would think this way. The point here is that **GIVE A DAMN** people don't think that any sum of money justifies lying at another's expense. Self-centered people are constantly thinking about themselves and what they can do for their own benefit, regardless of the effect it might have on others.

Here is another example that is cause for alarm. Several cities have installed red-light cameras at busy intersections to catch people running red lights or for speeding. If someone runs a red light, a picture of the license plate is taken and a ticket is mailed to his home. What's wrong with this? Nothing, but many people are up in arms because they consider it to be a violation of their rights. Seriously? Why? If you obey the law and don't run a red light nothing happens to you. So now people think that it's acceptable to run to a red light as long as they don't get caught? Isn't that their message? Where is the common sense logic here? I don't get it.

So now comes the next excuse: "This is just a money grab for the government!" Do people think that running a red light isn't illegal or dangerous? As long as you stop at the red light, you won't have a problem. It's those people that don't **GIVE A DAMN** that seemingly want the right to break traffic laws without suffering the consequence. People sue the government for installing these cameras (which are designed to catch people breaking the law) because they say it violates their rights and/or it's a money grab. They get caught red handed and yet even if they're guilty, they won't take responsibility for it. They don't **GIVE A DAMN** that this might be a safety issue. It is also an opportunity to make people more aware of their driving habits (it did for me because I got a camera speeding ticket for going 45 in a 30 MPH zone). Yet it has now become another example of people trying to get away with something they *know* is wrong; by making the excuse that cameras are violating their rights. It's ridiculous.

Here is another example that is even more ridiculous. While driving to work I heard an additional conversation about these same traffic cameras on the radio. An attorney called and stated that he was suing the city because he got a ticket for not coming to a complete stop when turning right on a red light. He stated on the air that he was *guilty* of the crime (yes, guilty!), but that he was suing the city because they were not able to identify him as being in the car, therefore, he should not have to pay the ticket. What? You admit your guilt and yet you are suing the city because they theoretically cannot identify you? What a terrible message. These are the kind of people that send bad messages to society; they are in it just for the publicity or the big pay day. This attorney should set an example, not give people more reasons to blame the system. People might have a legitimate case in some circumstances but this is ridiculous when he publicly admits he is flat out wrong.

We all know that there are truly bad people in this world. Yet, society is always trying to find an excuse for why these people act as they do. The person had a bad upbringing, was abused, did drugs, lacked education, lived in a rough neighborhood, or any other combination of misfortunes. So these excuses now give someone the right to do something bad? Seriously? How many times have you heard a lawyer bring up similar excuses in someone's defense? These are all unfortunate circumstances, and we should strive to eliminate them from our society. However, other than mental illness or impairment, these things do not affect one's cognitive ability to distinguish between right and wrong.

We have become masters of justification, which is another huge problem. How many times have you crumbled up a piece of paper, tossed it at a wastebasket and missed? Do you go back, pick it up and place it into the basket? Most people don't. It's just so much easier to walk away (because no one will notice and it is, after all, only a piece of paper). We justify it in our minds that it's no big deal. *It may not be a big deal, but that doesn't mean its right.* One problem with today's world is that people rarely think they have done anything wrong because they can justify their actions as being okay, or right in their own minds. Why do drug addicts steal? Because they have to support a habit, so it's justified to them. Deep down I believe they know it's wrong, but they have to do it to maintain their "high" and avoid painful withdrawals. We may not be familiar with this situation, but we are all familiar with this thought process. We miss the basket and don't go back to pick it up. Our justifications can range from "I am in a hurry," to "It's only a piece of paper," to "No one saw me anyway." But whatever the justification, none of them are valid. People who **GIVE A DAMN** don't think this way. If the paper doesn't make into the basket, pick it up and do the right thing. It saves someone else from having to do it!

Education

Education plays a very important role in the lives of people who **GIVE A DAMN**. Although the general trend in educational attainment in the USA amongst most all people between the years 1990 and 2014 has risen (1), there is a much greater need to focus on character education in our schools. It is just not happening adequately, and in some cases it's not happening at all. It is the best way to reach a majority of people since most children attend public or private school for at least some portion of their childhood. In the past, most of the character education we received occurred in our homes (and to a much lesser degree in schools). With a rise in the number of families with a single parent or with both parents working outside the home, parents are no longer spending as much time with their children. This lack of personal attention has taken a toll because children now spend less time (at home) interacting with their parents or guardians. Children spend eight hours or more at school, followed by some sort of after school program or activity while their parents are working. By the time children are home with their families, there is little time for dinner, completing homework and a bath, and much less on discussions related to manners, personal responsibility, accountability, compassion for others, etc. In families where children are able to come home right after school, much of their free time is spent watching television or playing video games. High quality TV shows and games that teach morals and positive values are next to impossible to find. It is a sad day when the most popular game among pre-adolescent males is called "Grand Theft Auto," and the goal is to steal cars and kill people to get what you want; let alone watching "The Walking Dead" or, "Here Comes Honey Boo Boo."

Not only is character education waning, the quality of a formal education is as well. This stems from two sources. One is the decreasing value that popular culture places on education, choosing instead to elevate the ideal of an "in the moment" lifestyle, which places good times and risky actions over discipline and study. The second cause is the greed and mismanagement of voters and politicians alike, who seem to cut education funding more and more every year. According to the OECD's Better Life Initiative for 2015 (2), U.S. middle schoolers are in the lower middle scores for math, science and reading. For adults, the scores in math were even worse, putting us behind all other nations except for Spain and Italy! The difference between the U.S. and high scoring countries such as Finland, Japan, and Korea, is that these countries chose to increase funding for education instead of cutting it.

An example of this disregard for education can be clearly illustrated in an example from my current home state of Louisiana. Several years ago (before 2009), the State of Louisiana passed the Stelly Plan, which eventually eliminated taxes on food and energy. To compensate for this loss of revenue, individual tax rates had to be raised. Then in 2009, Louisiana lawmakers wanted to repeal the Stelly tax, which would actually "reduce" people's taxes overall. However, such a move would cause a $200 million cut to higher education. There was a proposal to defer the repeal of the Stelly Plan so that this money could continue help fund higher education. Many people were against the deferral, including small businesses. So, no one would have had an increase in taxes compared to what they were already paying, yet a repeal would have a devastating effect on higher education.

I really don't get it other than this is a pure example of self-centered thinking. Many people were totally against deferring the repeal of the Stelly Plan. But why? Because they were only thinking of themselves, and the immediate benefit of more cash in their pockets. They were not thinking about how important education was for our State (let alone our country), especially when education is deteriorating at a rapid pace compared to other countries. I had an argument in front of about 40 people, stating that no one was getting a tax increase and that we really needed to improve the education level of our students. But most people were more concerned about what they could get back. The common theme was, "We already pay too much in taxes anyway!" So lawmakers, concerned more about votes than about the future of Louisiana's educational system, went along with the people. The Stelly Plan was abolished and our education system lost $200 million. I was pretty disturbed by the whole incident because it really showed how people think: "what's best for me?" instead of what might be best for others.

What's really interesting about those who prefer cutting education is their short-sightedness or short-term thinking. Although they think they're saving money, most economists will tell you that a country's quality of education has a direct impact on its Gross Domestic Product or GDP. A quality education boosts both the productivity and cognitive skills of a population, leading to a more resilient, innovative workforce. A more innovative workforce leads to greater progress in technology (an indirect problem which I discuss later) and other areas, which is a source of continuous economic growth for any country that can harness it. Studies have even suggested that a 10% increase in test scores (one of the best indicators of educational quality) raises average annual growth by at least .85 percentage points (3). When you have quality education at every level, it's not just students who win, its society as a whole that wins also.

So can the government help? Of course! The first step is for the government to spend its money more wisely (I know, that's a big joke). Let me explain. The government currently contributes to social welfare programs that provide financial support for a lot of people, but no motivation (or accountability) for people to actually better their lives. There is no finish line. They remain attached to programs that provide for their basic needs, but are never incentivized to strive for a greater goal. My suggestion is that the federal government put together programs for people to better their lives through education, but with a defined and definitive end. The government would provide people with *subsidized* (I know, it's a bad word) *education* so that individuals might make a contribution to society. In order to qualify for the program, the recipient would have to agree (through a written and signed contract) that once he completes the required education for a skill, there will be nothing more provided to him. As long as he remains able bodied and in control of his mental faculties he will be on his own. Through this method, the government is helping a person improve his life, not take care of him over a long period of time, unlike the majority of welfare programs today. If the person chooses not to make something out of what was provided for him then he should suffer the consequences of that decision. What's wrong with this?

Let me repeat. The government would provide free or low cost education to those who cannot afford it. At the same time, the person receiving this benefit needs to clearly understand that after he has completed his courses, it is his responsibility to get a job and the government can help him with that, too! However, there should be *an endpoint*, yes, <u>an endpoint</u> for all services provided by the government, after which the person becomes responsible for his own life. The person needs to fully understand that if he goes back to his old ways, he won't get any government support. Zero. Zip. Nada. There will be no more *ongoing* entitlements.

Personally, I think that both formal and character education are the key to really changing society's overall behavior, including preventing crime, and other major social ills. Here is the problem: when it comes to providing social and moral education outside the traditional classroom (I am not only talking about the home environment either), it is basically non-existent. We learn about subjects that we can name, such as math, science, and history; but we severely lack in a single, specific course that teaches manners, morals, responsibility, etiquette, character and how to really **GIVE A DAMN**. There are some schools, both public and private, that have attempted to teach "character" in the classroom. However, the message does not seem to get across adequately. In my opinion, it's because it's not being taught at an early enough age when children begin to form habits. It is not emphasized enough! Also, it is not enough to *tell* children how they should treat others; adults also need to *model* these behaviors.

The number one way to change a person's thought process is through direct instruction and modeling. To do this effectively, we have to start at a very early age. My suggestion is to make it a mandatory part of a curriculum as soon as a child begins school. Kindergarten through 8th grade courses would be called **GIVE A DARN**. These courses would teach common sense ideas that can be used in everyday life, such as proper and effective communication skills, ways to provide a helping hand, the importance of good manners, how to show gratitude, and much more. Don't tell me you can't teach this to kindergarten students either. I am tired of people finding excuses and reasons for why we can't do things rather than finding solutions to problems.

I am quite sure that many schools claim to emphasize these values, but this emphasis amounts to little more than motivational posters hung up on classroom walls and then ignored in practice. An actual annual course that provides credit would teach children how to truly incorporate this philosophy into their lives. Ideally, such courses would have a practical component as well. There are programs that sponsor special projects or experiences for middle and high school students that promote a **GIVE A DAMN** attitude towards others. However, these are optional and short-term opportunities. Having a student participate in one or even a handful of such experiences isn't likely to have the same impact as consistent coursework in character education. It would be ideal if every child had to participate every year in at least one service orientated course as part of their curriculum. I cannot emphasize this enough: it must start at a very early age. For older students who have already reached the later stages of their schooling, we need to start teaching what it means to **GIVE A DAMN** as soon as possible, in both high schools and universities. You might think that this is just another course that students take for easy credit (like physical education or home economics), but it is so much more than that. It's a service mantra philosophy of how we can contribute to making our world a better place to live and breathe, and to reduce violence. The only way to get people to understand this philosophy is to teach it in school, and make sure it is done as soon as children enter kindergarten.

Education, lack of education and one's socio-economic status can lead to misperceptions about a **GIVE A DAMN** attitude. Some people who are highly educated (and usually fairly wealthy) might be perceived as being arrogant and selfish because they have accumulated more personal property and opportunities to succeed. These people might not seem to **GIVE A DAMN** compared to others, because they have not given away all that they have to those who have less. Some wealthy people, even the well-educated, may not have experienced hard work or struggles because they have always had resources at their fingertips. These people may feel entitled to the lifestyle to which they have grown accustomed. On the other hand, less educated people and those who struggle financially often have fewer resources and must rely on the generosity of others or the government. People in such circumstances may feel entitled to financial help because things don't come as easily to them as they do for others. A sense of entitlement can get in the way for both the rich and the poor, and often prevents people from helping others in whatever ways they can (more on this in the Wealth section). No matter our level of education or the financial resources at our disposal, we can all do our part to **GIVE A DAMN**. There is no excuse.

(1) https://nces.ed.gov/fastfacts/display.asp?id=27
(2) http://www.oecdbetterlifeindex.org/topics/education/
(3) Education Quality and Economic Growth. The World Bank; written by Eric A. Hanushek and Ludger Wobmann, 2007.

CHAPTER 4

Social and Cultural Ills - It's Another Problem

Institutions have certainly played their part in perpetuating a don't **GIVE A DAMN** mentality. However, the larger issue may be found in popular culture, and the waning of traditional values. Here we will explore the problems that arise within our homes that we can only solve through changing our own habits and attitudes.

Religion

We can no longer openly practice our religious beliefs, because doing so might offend others. Although our country was founded as, "One nation under God," certain individuals and factions want to take the word "God" out of our society every chance they get. It's as if these individuals are taking this personally and think that everything is directed at them. When has that ever been the case? It hasn't been for hundreds of years and now it becomes a problem? In my opinion, these people simply want to feel special or recognized in some way. Inventing false forms of persecution is a great way to attract sympathy or attention that they would not otherwise ever get.

You rarely see or hear any mention of God these days, with the exception of being part of a religious institution or in some very old public buildings. Perhaps this is part of our problem. Yet, I firmly believe the real problem is this trend of individuals taking anything found in the public sphere as a direct and personal attack on oneself. It's just not so.

No longer can school children say prayers in our public schools, and Christmas and Easter parties are forbidden because it is supposedly "offensive." This is despite the fact that the same people who take offense at these parties would have no problem with a religious majority in any other country publicly celebrating their religious holidays. Whether it is Christian students celebrating Easter, Muslim students celebrating Eid a-Adha, or Hindu students celebrating Diwali, none of these festivities are meant to force religion on anyone. They are simply a way to honor a country's traditions and culture, and to share that pride with others. In America, these traditions happen to be predominately Christian, but it is the same concept anywhere else in the world. Those who do not share the same beliefs can still take joy in the celebrations, or at least take them as a learning experience.

Most everyone has heard about Tim Tebow. He was the 2010 Heisman trophy winner. He graduated from the University of Florida and went on to play in the National Football League. Tim is very spiritual and has demonstrated this through his actions, both on and off the football field. Some people are offended by his displays of spirituality, but why? Tebow is either thanking God for his accomplishments and/or praying to help him accomplish something. Why should anyone be upset by that? His actions are not being directed at anyone personally, but people act like this is the case, and therefore they find his behavior offensive. He has no ulterior motive. In fact, it seems as though most of the controversy surrounding Tim Tebow is the fact that he is one of the most uncontroversial athletes on the planet. He has no major vices, no criminal record, and practices the values that he preaches. It is as if he is holding up a mirror of what society *could* or *should* be, and those on the other side don't like what they see. Now, if Tebow were to come up and shove a Bible in your face that would be offensive or even abusive because it would be directed at you, but that is not what he is doing. No one should be offended by Tim Tebow praying. Again, you don't have to agree with his actions, but people who are offended by this and try to do something to prevent it from happening are part of a bigger problem.

The farther you go back in time the more people were inclined to **GIVE A DAMN**. Our founding fathers are a perfect example. Without going into detail, the Constitution clearly showed that our founding fathers were more concerned with others than themselves. People back then had faith in those beliefs. But as time moves on, these beliefs seem to be changing with the masses, or are twisted to accommodate people's self-interests. People today are often so caught up in furthering their personal agenda that they want to impose their own causes onto others. They take things personally and therefore want to make changes to society as a whole. Usually the changes are based on the best interests of only a few.

Think back to the case that was mentioned in the previous section in which the ACLU campaigned against a picture of Jesus hanging in a Slidell court. No one complained about it for years until an unnamed defendant claimed it was violating his freedom of religion. Then the ACLU jumped on the bandwagon and it was immediately all over the papers. Even after the court expanded the display to include many other religious and historical figures, the ACLU still took issue. Now, all pictures have been removed from the wall. Give me a break. Then again, how about the four "Confederate" monuments that have been on display for a huge number of years in New Orleans? It's part of history. Now there is a movement to remove those from public display because it *now* offends people. After all these years, the monuments are now offensive? They were not put up to offend people. They were put up to honor history. But now they have *become offensive*. If you don't like it, don't look at them. Better yet, let's have the people decide by taking a vote where the majority wins! It's just a common sense simple solution that everyone would have to live with, just like in an election.

Family Values

A mother was preparing pancakes for her sons, Kevin, 5 and Ryan 3. The boys began to argue over who would get the first pancake. Their mother saw the opportunity for a moral lesson. She said, "If Jesus were sitting here, He would say, "Let my brother have the first pancake, I can wait." Kevin turned to his younger brother and said, "Ryan, you be Jesus!" Sure, this is supposed to be funny but the message is pretty clear.

I remember growing up and how I wanted to be first in everything (especially over my twin sister). Most kids probably do the same because they don't know any better at a young age. For instance, my Mom had a steak bone for a neighbor's dog and my sister and I were fighting over who was going to give it to him. We were eight years old at the time and we were both climbing concrete steps at the same time to get the bone. She was ahead of me so I pulled her down to get ahead. She landed on her chin and required six stitches. I should have let my sister give the dog the bone and my opportunity would have come later. Because I didn't **GIVE A DAMN**, my sister got hurt. But at my age I did not know any better. It is natural for young children to exhibit selfish behavior, but our responsibility as parents is to lead by example, and help children understand the importance (and also the reward) of putting others first. If we don't teach our children this lesson early, society will certainly pay for it later on.

Sadly, our version of tough love is basically gone. Today when a child hits 18, he is on his own. When I was 18, my parents were still very much involved with my life; they guided me, helped me get into college, helped me with medical issues and much more. Once kids turn 18 parents cannot get information on their children without their permission, whereas 20 years ago it wasn't a problem. My thought is that if parents declare a child on their tax return as a dependent and fully support him and his needs, then they should have access to his school and medical records, with or without his consent. If the child is totally on his own, parents don't need his information anyway. Society has created an environment in which parents cannot assist children like they used to, and in some cases the child does not want it either, which I think is pretty sad.

Furthermore, this idea about child abuse has gone way too far. I am all about protecting children from being abused and there are certainly limits. However, there is a difference between child abuse and child punishment. Spanking a child for doing something wrong is not child abuse, it's called a consequence for doing something wrong, also known as "tough love." When a child says, "If you spank or strike me, I am going to sue you for abuse," there is something inherently wrong with this relationship between parent and child, and there are much deeper issues to be addressed.

When parents exemplify a **GIVE A DAMN** attitude, their actions rub off on their children, even if it might not seem apparent at first. For example, I had a friend who was complaining to me about his lazy 22 year old son who lived with him. He did laundry but only his own, he never cleaned up after himself, he took clean dishes out of the dishwasher but never emptied it completely; he never cleaned his bathroom and more. I told him to make an effort to **GIVE A DAMN** towards his son but not to the point where he would become submissive. I told him that it might take awhile but the seed on how to **GIVE A DAMN** would eventually germinate. Eventually it did, but not until he was on his own. I guess he realized that in order to really succeed in life you need to **GIVE A DAMN** on a consistent basis. Everyone has a **GIVE A DAMN** seed inside. These seeds might take longer to germinate in some people versus others. It just depends on the environment and the amount of nurturing that the seeds receive. But the seed is there for germinating!

Although there are always challenges and difficulties in raising a child in today's world, we actually **GIVE A DAMN** more for kids than anyone else. Why? Because children cannot fend for themselves, and are still learning and developing, so we take care of them. If we were to show children how to **GIVE A DAMN** over and over again, it would become a learned response and an instinctive part of a child's wiring of the brain. It would be a gift we would give to our children: our learned **GIVE A DAMN** behavior. The subconscious mind knows how to **GIVE A DAMN**. We just don't execute it consciously. Can we teach ourselves and others how to **GIVE A DAMN**? I think we can, and it's through our actions. Instead of telling our children to "share" and "take turns" and "if you can't say something nice, don't say it at all," we have to demonstrate and show to our children that we *do* these good things, and point out the positive effects our actions have on others. People can learn to **GIVE A DAMN** if they are simply aware of the positive effects it has on people. In addition to dedicated and focused instruction on character education, perhaps the best way to instill the **GIVE A DAMN** attitude in our children is for adults to model this same attitude. If every adult in a child's life is doing the right thing, the child will learn to do the right thing as well.

Chivalry used to be a big part of family values in the past. Personally, I think it's on its way out, or has been out for some time. Chivalry can be summed up as thinking of and doing things for other people (and it's not just a male thing either). Chivalry is as easy as opening a car door for someone, getting up so that another (woman, elderly etc.) person might sit down on a bus, letting someone get in an elevator before you, holding a door open, or helping someone walk across the street. These are simple small gestures that show respect for other people, no matter who they are. Another thing lost in today's society is the teaching of etiquette. Good proper etiquette is a **GIVE A DAMN** trait. What happened to the words "please" and "thank you?" These simple words are missing more and more from today's society.

As I was traveling to work one day, I heard news on the radio about a person who was crossing a long bridge over a body of water and threw two kittens out of a car window. One of the kittens managed to survive as it was found in a drain. The other did not. The story was all over the news. How could anyone commit such a heinous act? The next morning the radio talk show host brought the subject up for people to call in and discuss. The question was, "How can anyone even *think* about doing something so barbaric?" The talk show host commented that once the person was found he should go straight to jail (for a long time). One guy called in and said that as a youngster he did similar idiotic things but has since reformed his ways because he found God. At the same time, the caller said that he thought people were just inherently evil and that these kinds of things were ingrained into our psyche; it was human nature. What? I was fuming, not only because of the kitten incident, but because the caller said we are innately evil in nature. I don't believe that at all. Society is just too self-centered. People (especially those who would throw kittens out of a speeding car) just don't **GIVE A DAMN** about anyone but themselves. Were the kittens mean? Were they too expensive to care for? If either were true, the right thing would have been to give the kittens up for adoption, not throw them out of a car window going 60 miles per hour! Is this just not common sense?

Would anyone think about throwing his own personal and loving pet out of a car, or for that matter, a child? I hope not! Once we love something, it is our natural instinct to protect it and fight for it, to **GIVE A DAMN**. Maybe the kitten thrower justified his actions based on not being able to take care of the kittens, but throwing them out of a car window is not the solution. There was no consideration for the well being of those kittens. This type of self-centeredness is ruining our society and it's becoming more rampant every day.

Wealth

This is a pretty sensitive subject. Sometimes the wealthier you are, the less you **GIVE A DAMN**, because you have learned that money can take care of anything (again, this is not true for everyone as I know individuals who are very generous with their money). Kudos to you who are reading this book and have been very generous with your wealth, both in time and money – Thank you! But here is a different example. When I used to run a non-profit organization, we paid for a speaker to come to New Orleans to talk about Entrepreneurship and Innovation to our members (this was actually the very first time we had ever paid for a speaker). This person was an icon and had made millions on the Internet. We contracted him for a $5,000 fee to do a 90 minute speaking luncheon. The normal fee was $25,000 (which I found a little absurd), so this was a great deal for our organization. We did have to pay all his travel expenses (air, hotel and food) from Boston to New Orleans. The contract stated that his flight had to be first class and fully refundable. When they emailed us and said it would cost between $1,500 and $2,100 (round trip) I was a bit shocked. We then went online and saw that we could book the same first class flight for $800. I could not understand. I don't think they cared what it cost (since they were not paying for it) but to us it was significant. Personally, I spend other people's money like it's my own, always trying to save where I can. Should it matter that they discounted the speaker fee for us? Sure, and I was grateful, but shouldn't that line of thinking be consistent? If you focus on what you can do for others rather than yourself, this shouldn't be an issue. We were a non-profit group. Could he justify that since he saved us $20,000 for the speaker's fee, he could take a more expensive flight? Sure. But why? I think that many people who have money sometimes forget that others are not so financially independent. Not all of them, but enough to be significant.

Another example that demonstrates a don't **GIVE A DAMN** attitude was during the hundreds of events that I planned when working for my former non-profit group. In almost every instance, we asked people to register online for an event so that we would know how many people would attend, and therefore we would know how much food to order (which was free to the attendee). This is especially important when doing a Lunch and Learn session. Invariably, we got many people who registered and simply did not show up. They didn't even notify us that they weren't coming! We got the registration, paid for a meal and they didn't even show up! Wasn't it just common courtesy for them to tell us if they were not going to come, regardless of whether it was a free event or not? Was it just laziness or a lack of manners, or both? How would they feel if they were hosting the event, had 50 registrations and no one showed up? It is all driven by an internal thinking process and not thinking about how their actions might affect others. **GIVE A DAMN** people don't do this. I could understand if it was an emergency, but these no-shows aren't a rarity, they happen all the time.

I believe there are many categories of people who generally don't **GIVE A DAMN** and there are probably two that stand out the most: those who have lots of money and those who have very little (now mind you, I want to strongly make this point again, and I do it throughout the book; there are exceptions to my generalizations, as there are in every situation, and I know lots of wealthy people who are humbled and very generous). People who have lots of money can really buy anything they want. The very rich sometimes don't always care about what they do and the effect their money might have on others. They may be insulated from many of the challenges that other people face, which they just might not realize. This "out of sight, out of mind" perspective may be a factor in whether the very wealthiest people in our society **GIVE A DAMN** or not. People with lots of money might also be consumed by the love of money, causing them to lose sight of what is most important in life.

On the other end of the spectrum, very poor people generally don't **GIVE A DAMN** for opposite reasons. They might feel oppressed, therefore believing that society owes them, and society (government) should take care of them. They feel they are "entitled" to receive help instead of looking for ways that they might be able to help themselves or others. So what about people in the middle? At the end of the day, it is all about who you are. The middle class has the same challenges, they just don't necessarily have the same extreme belief boundaries of the wealthy and the poor that would influence how they do or do not **GIVE A DAMN**.

If I told people to **GIVE A DAMN** and by doing so they could make 15 times their annual earnings (and let's say I had statistics to prove it), do you think they would? Absolutely! The problem with this type of thinking is that they would do it only for the money, meaning that they are thinking about themselves. It is still a self-centered attitude. Sure it should be a factor when you have to earn a living and need to take care of your family, but that becomes the difference. It's your family that is most important. We need to think outside our own internal-thinking personal domain as a pure way to **GIVE A DAMN**.

As I have noted earlier, I dislike the phrase: "That's not my job." You work for a company and respond to a request for help by saying, "That's not my job?" This is the ultimate message that reveals who you are. This is what a truly self-centered person would say. They don't **GIVE A DAMN** about helping anyone unless it serves their best interest. If they can personally benefit, then they will help. This type of attitude is becoming far too pervasive.

I came across a sign outside a New Orleans, LA business that read, "Are you proud of your work today?" It really makes you think. You see, when people do their jobs without truly caring about the effort they put in to it, they only do what they are supposed to do. No more than that, and if possible, less. Corporate America typically does not empower people to go the extra mile and **GIVE A DAMN** (and I will state it again, there are always exceptions to the rule). Many organizations don't encourage creativity or individuality to serve others. These are 9 to 5 people, it doesn't matter what needs to be done, they leave at 5:00 PM sharp. These people are self-centered. They only have jobs because it pays them money. This is sad because the statistics today show that most people are unhappy with their jobs. People should engage in a job that makes a difference; the money is extra or just icing on the cake. People need to take pride in their work, which seems to becoming more rare than common. Sometimes we encounter a person who says, "I love my job *and* I get paid for doing it!" They think that because they get paid for something that they love to do, "it's unbelievable!" Even if you are in a job that you truly don't like, if you practice the **GIVE A DAMN** attitude, you just might like it better. The more we care about something, the more interesting it becomes.

I was shopping and needed bar stools. They were $20 each and two came in a box. When the cashier scanned the bar code, I got charged for one stool. The cashier simply thought that the scanned item was the total price. I knew what he had done. In the past, I would have tried to get a "free bar stool," but it was wrong. I told the guy and he rang up the second stool. I could have easily gotten away with it if I'd wanted to, but I didn't. I think people generally make wrong decisions if they feel that they can get away with it. To them, not getting caught is a victory unto itself. It happens when people commit a crime, steal, tell a lie, or hurt others in numerous other ways. But it will always, and I mean *always,* come back to bite you, sooner or later. The truth always wins. **GIVE A DAMN** people tell the truth. **GIVE A DAMN** people don't care who is watching them. **GIVE A DAMN** people always do the right thing. **GIVE A DAMN** people take responsibility. **GIVE A DAMN** people care. **GIVE A DAMN** people think about other people, not just themselves. If you could get everyone to **GIVE A DAMN** we could leave our doors open at night, keep our cars unlocked, and walk the streets at any hour. You get the point?

Technology

This is a big topic for me because I basically grew up in technology. I worked for IBM for more 13 years and ran a non-profit technology council for more than 10 years. However, one of the biggest problems in today's society is that direct interaction between people has decreased over the past several years. This is absolutely due to our ever expanding dependence on technology. Now you might say technology, especially social media and mobile apps, has allowed us to communicate with more people than ever before. In one sense, this is true. However, face to face human interaction has decreased immensely due to the rapid onslaught of technology and the technology devices we use every day. We can reach out to more people than ever before, and yet our interpersonal skills are declining. Communication through email and texting can be interpreted differently than its intent. Plus, it is much easier to avoid or misrepresent a situation through email than on the phone or face to face. I have friends who tell me they would rather text than talk on the phone. And although neither texting nor talking on the phone is face-to-face, isn't verbal communication better than sending a text when it comes to interacting with someone? It's more personal. Many expressions conveyed through vocal tone, or even pauses in speech are lost in text messages.

Worst of all, this increase in digital communication makes it much easier for people to avoid real world social interaction. If you reduce the desire for someone to interact directly with people in society, you reduce their ability to care or think about others. And I'm not just basing this off my own intuition; there are scientific studies to back it up! A 2010 study by the University of Michigan demonstrated how college student's scores in empathy have been steadily declining since 1990 (1). This has been accompanied by a sharp rise in narcissism, and "self" oriented goals. In 2006, 64% of 18 years olds surveyed said that making money was the most important goal of all! (2). Most social scientists agree that increased "screen time" is a contributing factor to this thought process. Whether in the form of obsessively updating profile pictures, texting through family dinners or being absorbed in violent video games, all this new technology is taking its toll. And guess what? Lack of empathy in individuals is directly correlated to criminal acts, especially violent ones (3). We don't notice the effects of a generation growing up with less empathy now (although you can feel it starting to emerge). But what about 20 years from now? The balance of direct interaction in society has tipped to greater communication with others but at the expense of direct personal contact or direct interaction. Our interactions with others are *increasing in quantity*, but are *declining in quality*.

Society has become so technology driven and things have become so automated that we don't have that human touch like we did in the 80's, 90's (or even before then). Instead of calling someone, you send a text. Instead of writing someone, you send an email. Spelling and grammar no longer matter and you can say pretty much whatever you want, as long as you insert a "JK", "LOL" or, "smiley face," or many other types of emoticons at the end of a statement.

I was involved with my daughter in an incident at a major superstore that epitomizes how people act in today's society. We were shopping for school supplies and we had a cart with about 20 items in it. Due to the number of people in the store, we would frequently leave our cart (out of people's way) to walk around and get supplies. We would then come back and put them in the cart. When we got back to our cart, a lady was taking out all of our items and putting them into her empty cart. I asked her, "What are you doing?" She then appeared very flustered and began putting our items back into our cart while sputtering, "My cart was squeaking." What she was doing was switching carts so she would not hear the squeaking of her own cart. My daughter and I looked at each other in disbelief. Was it too hard or time-consuming to get another cart? I cannot imagine it taking more than one minute to do so! The right thing would have been to go back to the front of the store and replace the cart, not steal someone else's! I was shocked. The funny part is that we passed this same lady again in the frozen food section, and guess what? Her cart wasn't squeaking! Maybe she did go to the front of the store and get another cart. But my suspicion was that she had probably gotten away with it at someone else's expense. Totally mindboggling!

Let me close this section by stating that I firmly believe that far too many people are way too concerned about protecting their "turf." I am not referring to "physical turf" like property or what you possess. "Turf" here refers to your non-physical personal interests. It is the domain you have in your mind, meaning you are constantly making sure that you have the best of everything. It's ego driven. People who do not **GIVE A DAMN** will step on anyone that gets in the way of this self-centered domain pursuit. What people don't realize is that most people can help you rather than hurt you. If you are constantly protecting your turf and not doing things for people, over time you will lose friends, trust, lack of people wanting to help you, confidence in yourself, your smile and all the other truly good things in life. It perpetuates itself and gets worse over time. That's when you start feeling the pain.

(1) Michigan News, University of Michigan. Empathy: <u>College Students Don't have as Much as They Used to.</u> Diane Swanbrow, May 27, 2010

(2) http://www.people-press.org/files/legacy-pdf/300.pdf; The Pew Research Center, January 9, 2006. Andrew Kohut, Director.

(3) http://www.psmag.com/books-and-culture/dark-side-empathy-91399, Pacific Standard, Tom Jacobs, September, 26, 2014

Media

It won't be easy to change the way most people think and inspire them to consider the needs of others before their own. After all, many of the messages we receive from the media do anything *but* support a **GIVE A DAMN** attitude. Our role models today in pop music, television, movies, fashion, and professional sports suggest that the way to be truly successful and happy in life is to be very thin, have multiple houses, drive fast cars, abuse drugs and alcohol, engage in promiscuous behavior and wear a lot of expensive flashy jewelry or clothing. The people that our children look up to and the media that surrounds them suggests that bad language, and a self-absorbed lifestyle will get you lots of attention....never mind if it is negative!

In the 1940's, Americans banded together with Victory Gardens, scrap metal drives and inspirational music. In the 1950's, we watched shows like *Lassie* and *Father Knows Best* as a family, and then perhaps discussed the lessons learned from these types of programs. In the 1960's and 1970's, *Andy Griffith*, *Little House on the Prairie* and *The Brady Bunch* helped teach us important morals and values, and how to express those values through our behavior. There were positive messages delivered in folk music. There were positive messages in achieving equal rights for all people, regardless of gender, race or physical challenges.

Today these shows would probably be considered "cheesy." But, since then, one can trace a steady shift in the message. Young girls began feeling insecure about their bodies when compared to Barbie dolls and airbrushed magazine models. Little boys starting to believe that tattoos, big muscles and gold teeth are the things that make one successful as a grown up. Seemingly the message received by most everyone (young and old alike) is that honest hard work is just too much work! Our music now suggests that we should all "Get Our Shine On," and try to "Get Lucky." Current musicians tell us that our elders and people in law enforcement "Can't Hold Us," and that "We

Can't Stop…We Won't Stop" (drinking and doing drugs and being overtly sexual in public). One interesting way to illustrate this is the change in song titles from pop songs in the 1950s to those today. In the 50's, the five most commonly found words in billboard song titles were "Christmas," "Penny," "Mambo," "Red Nosed," and "Three." As for the 2010s? The most popular words are "We", "Hell," "Yeah," "F*ck," and "Die." Quite a change, don't you think?

Certainly there are celebrities and athletes who use their fame to raise money and awareness for charities and other worthy causes. Many adopt needy children, and make very positive changes in our world. But too often, these good deeds take a back seat to the more risky, rude and obnoxious actions of many self-absorbed celebrities with seemingly insatiable egos. Plus, our children have more access to negative behaviors than ever before. The Internet and television provide a constant stream of activities related to famous people and their inappropriate behaviors. And the ordinary citizens that we *choose* to promote to celebrity status in viral videos and reality shows are generally the ones with the least amount of education, manners and class. To be in and out of rehab is now a sign that you have arrived! This obsession with fame has shifted to a much darker side as well. News programs are full of stories about shootings in schools, movie theatres, and malls. Many of these shooters are seeking the news coverage and notoriety that they see as the ultimate achievement. Our political leaders engage in sexual misconduct, fraud and theft. They lie and cheat and lie some more. Voters seek immediate information via text and the Internet, and as long as that information is fast, its accuracy is secondary. Entertainment is designed to provide cheap laughs rather than provoke thought. Many young people spend their time sharing "Selfies" with hundreds of "friends" on a myriad of social media sites. Yes, in a society where it is acceptable to be impatient, rude, selfish, overweight, drunk, lazy and ignorant; it will be a real challenge to incite change. But, it is not impossible.

CHAPTER 5

GIVE A DAMN and Violence

One would have a hard time arguing against the assertion that to-day's society is increasing in violence. It seems to me that more and more individuals are placing less of a value on human life, whether it's their own or that of others. This seeming disregard for life takes many forms: terrorism, gang violence, and mass shootings being the most notable examples. This is not to say that there has never been violence in the past (a quick glance at a history book easily disproves that!), but it seems to be entering a new territory. New forms of violence, especially terror, are escalating and spiraling out of control. Some people would argue that human beings are naturally violent and we have simply curbed our natural inclinations in order to create a functional society. To them, it seems we are only slightly more advanced than chimpanzees. I don't think so. Do you honestly think that any new born baby is born to be violent? Do babies have violence already predisposed in their blood when they are born? Anyone with common sense would think not. Furthermore, what role does the environment play in how a newborn learns behavior? A ton! So the question is: Are we little more than animals living within a civilization, or have we simply ceased to **GIVE A DAMN** about others? I think it's the latter.

There is absolutely no way that humans are born with an instinct to hurt or kill others. How can there be any benefit in doing this? Each day you can find countless instances in which humans have shown great displays of kindness, altruism, and elevation of spirit; all **GIVE A DAMN** characteristics. How in the world could our species have lasted over the past 200,000 years without the instinct to care about others? Humans have the greatest minds in the world. There have been many instances in the past when some twisted "leader" or faction has tried to take over the world and failed. If you were to look at these failed occurrences, none of these so called leaders or groups had a **GIVE A DAMN** attitude. And guess what, they all eventually failed! Most people eventually saw through them, and rejected the ideals of those who were bloodthirsty or power hungry, which has certainly been the cause of many revolutions throughout history.

However, times have changed, and as noted before, the rapid growth of technology has played a huge and detrimental role in our behavior. I am not suggesting that technology is bad overall, but in this case, it is. There seems to be a growing "cancer" of apathy these days, which has led many people to forget how to care for others. Many people have simply ceased (or never learned) to **GIVE A DAMN** about any life other than their own, and sometimes not even their own. Sometimes this may seem harmless to all but the person afflicted, such as the case of many young ones who are wasting their lives on videogames. But it can also become deadly, leading people to think that their worldview or frustration merits violent behavior, such as taking the life of another. I believe this is one of the contributing factors to three of most extreme manifestations of violence today: gang violence, rampage killings, and terrorism. And yet, we have almost become desensitized by all the violence we see on TV, in video games, in movies and the world in general. Years ago we would react in disbelief to violent actions or behaviors, such as shootings or bombings. Now it seems like we say, "It happened again," and without much emotion. We just cannot consider such behaviors as being acceptable or even expected. Simply put, common sense tells me these acts are a result of people who just don't **GIVE A DAMN**. Their drive has become 100% internally driven. So, if we can change people's thinking, can we help change their behavior? I sure hope so and I hope it's not too late either.

In recent years, the United States has seen an upswing in violent crime. Thirty-five large US cities have seen spikes in the murder rate (violent crime) from 2014 to 2015 (1). Although many of those involved with crimes have been affiliated with gangs or drugs, it is easy to see that the problem goes way beyond these areas. Officials say that it is no longer just the stereotypical gang wars fought over territory or robberies that sparked these killings. More often than not, the motives behind these killings have been centered on trivial (and what I would call ego driven) circumstances, such as maintaining one's status or worth. It's ironic to think that the most commonly cited reasons for violent behavior are based on trivial arguments! Yes, a simple argument that somehow escalated to hatred and then murder. If you think about it, the majority of murders in this country occur because two people get into an argument over something simplistic such as money, status, or a relationship. It seems petty to us, but in the violent behavioral mind, the fear of losing "face" is a huge blow to the psyche or ego.

I firmly believe this is exactly what happened with beloved and former New Orleans Saints football great, Will Smith, who was murdered in 2016. Here is a tragic case where something bubbled up, and a heated argument ensued that caused the perpetrator to shoot and kill Will Smith. One of the two involved in this incident should have taken control and defused the situation but neither did because their egos got in the way. It became a "me versus him" mentality. Someone had to win and a life was taken. It's just so sad that an outstanding 34 year old former football player with a wife and kids was tragically gunned down for no reason at all.

The thought process by both Will Smith and his murderer was probably, "He is not going to do that to me and get away with it!" People that don't **GIVE A DAMN** usually want to win at someone else's expense. And I will emphasize this again that it's an ego self-driven type of mentality. They're not very good sports when they lose, either. Everyone wants immediate satisfaction by winning. What people don't realize is that by giving, you will win by doing the right thing (even though it might not give you immediate satisfaction). Why is it that someone always has to win, and if they don't, they have to cause harm?

The problem is that this type of behavior seems to be a frightening and growing trend. Our culture is becoming more and more accustomed to using violence as a solution, regardless of how small the issue may be. There has to be a way to reign in this culture of violence. It is in no way an easy fix because changing a mindset is a monumental task. So my hope is that this book can offer some solutions, or at least be a starting point in the solution. Am I a dreamer? Sure, but we have to start somewhere and why not now!

Most would agree that our society has shifted towards placing a greater value on obtaining wealth and status, no matter the consequence. This often serves as an excuse or justification for everything under the sun. Some children, especially those who are disadvantaged, join gangs at a young age in order to obtain an image of power or wealth. They generally feel they have no means to obtain these things legally so they turn to crime instead. It is their way of seeking immediate *short-term* gratification for doing something "cool." They are willing to take that risk of crime and not worry about the consequence. So they begin the journey of petty crimes, which eventually grows into riskier crimes and then to extreme violence, leading to imprisonment or even death. They don't **GIVE A DAMN** about what happens to them or others. Sadly, this process starts at a very young age, and usually ends at a young age, too. Did you know that the median age of those killed in gang violence is 23? And the median age of those convicted of murder is 27 (2)? These are pretty sad statistics.

In my opinion, there needs to be a heavy emphasis on what it means to **GIVE A DAMN**. Our youth needs to understand the process and demands of what it takes to work hard and to obtain earned wealth, and that just doesn't happen overnight. They must understand that hard work, no matter how tedious it may seem at first, is a much better (and ultimately more profitable) choice than taking the quick, dirty, life threatening route. Too many young people are captivated by songs about designer clothes and private jets, the opulent Instagram feeds of their favorite celebrities, and the million dollar mansions of reality (or actually unreality) TV. They associate these lavish displays of wealth with respect and power, and don't realize that most of it is fantasy. The media (especially social media) constantly feeds this kind of sensationalism to our youth. Viewers only see the end result and they have no idea that this doesn't happen overnight. They are never taught that success is the result of hard work and not the intricate production techniques that go into creating an image of extreme wealth. As such, they want instant gratification and therefore aspire to grab a piece of the pie, as quickly and easily (and falsely) as they imagine their favorite stars have done. It's a bad message but it sure has a major impact on ratings. Ah yes, ratings. More ratings, more dollars, more profits; and usually at the expense of doing the right thing. Some would say that people who watch TV know it's fantasy. That may be true for the older generation but not for the younger kids because they are so impressionable. Popular culture in its current form teaches nothing about how to **GIVE A DAMN**.

Later on in the book, I discuss and make some suggestions about how parents can **GIVE A DAMN**, and teach their children the value of doing the right thing at a *very* early age. They need to demonstrate both through their words and actions that wealth and status are earned, and could possibly fade, but being a good person never does. Unfortunately, the pressures of making a living often means both parents have to work long hours. As a result, parents are sometimes too busy or distracted to monitor their children's activities. The freer the reign that a child has regarding rules, structure, and consequences, the more they will test what they can get away with. Pushing boundaries is a normal part of growing up. Often parents don't realize their child has gone down the wrong path until it is too late. I do realize that families with two working parents cannot always be there for their children but I do believe that teaching kids how to contribute to society (the real reason why we are born) should be a focus and a priority. A lot of times it's not. However, if the parents cannot always be present, the least they can do is instill the right values in their children's minds. So even if the parents are not around, the child knows and does the right thing. If they don't, the child will suffer the consequence of his parent's negligence later on in life.

Random Acts of Violence

The United States is one of top countries in the world when it comes to mass shooting incidents when compared to other developed countries (3). Although we often dismiss the perpetrators as merely mentally ill or having suffered some type of traumatic experience in their life, this phenomenon is becoming all too common; almost like an epidemic. There has to be something more to it. I am not discounting the fact that active shooters could have mental health issues that drive them to murder people for no apparent reason. What I am saying is that there has to be something else going on that turns these mental health issues deadly. There are other issues going on the brain that somehow feed a drive towards violence.

There is a point that I want to emphasis here before continuing. I do believe that some people have unbalanced brains (chemical imbalance), meaning their behavior is disruptive because of how the brain reacts and operates in certain situations. Many times a person cannot help himself and the actions in which he or she partakes, so the brain needs some type of medication to bring it into balance. Medication does a lot to help these chemical imbalances, but it is not a cure-all. It can help the biological side of the problem, but not the moral side. I sure wish society would treat mental health issues the same way we treat physical health issue like high cholesterol or high blood pressure. The physical body has an imbalance that medication treats and we are okay with that, yet we see it a whole lot differently when it comes to mental health (or brain) imbalances that we fail to treat like physical conditions. Fix the brain imbalance and you help fix crime.

As I have stated earlier, I am not a psychologist nor do I have *any* background in medicine. So I am sure many mental health care professionals will think that my **GIVE A DAMN** ideas are blasphemy or stupid or just can't work. But if you sit back and think, the ideas and theories I have are based on simple common sense. It's the KISS principle: *keep it simple stupid.* So here is my theory on most random acts of violence: random acts (or for that matter, any act of violence) are based on the desire of the perpetrator(s) to seek fame, glory, or recognition; and the willingness to go to any length to get it. These perpetrators feel that they have been in the shadows all their lives and no one cares about them. Often, the only attention they ever receive is negative: "You're not good enough, you're stupid, you're lazy," and so on. They begin to associate negative attention as being the only way for them to get noticed. And what's a great way to gain the ultimate form of negative attention? In extreme cases, it's having one's face plastered across TV or the front pages of newspapers after having murdered many people. These people do not consider or care about the consequences of their actions when it comes to other human beings. They don't **GIVE A DAMN** as to who gets hurt or dies as long as they receive the "ultimate" coverage. And once they finish their act, they often commit suicide, likely seeing themselves as going out in a final blaze of notoriety or glory.

So how does the media play a role in all of this? By exploiting and sensationalizing spree killings. Sure they have to cover it, but frankly they don't **GIVE A DAMN** about the excessive coverage provided for this kind of violence. Why? Because it attracts viewers and ratings, and the better the ratings, the more money it will generate. Does such sensationalized coverage attract copycat acts? Commons sense says, *positively*! Social scientists at the University of Arizona have theorized that excessive news coverage of mass shootings has a contagious effect for 13 days (when coverage begins to die down), leading to more potential shootings within that time period (4). Continued coverage of violent acts has served as a model on which others with the same sick mindset can shape their own actions. Both Seung Hui Cho, the Virginia Tech shooter (April, 2007), and Adam Lanza, perpetrator of the Sandy Hook massacre (December 2012) were fascinated by the Columbine shootings, with Cho even going so far as to praise the shooters as "martyrs" in his final manifesto. James Holmes, the Colorado movie theater shooter (July, 2012) was quoted during his trial as saying, "At least I'm remembered for doing something." There is obviously something going on in a person's psyche other than mental illness for them to say something like this. That something is a thirst for attention regardless of the cost to others.

One possible contributor to bad behavior is what we have accepted as normal in today's society, and which technology has made so readily available: violent videogames that focus on killing and destruction, violent movies, pornography, ultimate fighter programs and more. Years ago we would abhor such programs or ideas, but now they have become commonplace and even celebrated. Social scientists refer to these types of programs as "cultural zones of exception," in which people can temporarily disregard the norms of civilized society in order to briefly live out their darkest fantasies. And this is not supposed to affect us in any way? Media enables people to view acts of violence without having to suffer the consequences of being witnesses or participants in real life (talk about putting a spin on something). Does this pass the common sense test? Absolutely not. In time, people who frequently partake in this kind of "violent" entertainment become desensitized to it, requiring more and more extreme experiences to "jump start" that feeling (5). The more desensitized they become (as noted earlier), the more normal it seems to them, and eventually they acquire a sort of learned behavior. This eventually becomes an obsession or addiction, which can sometimes become deadly. Again, I am not a doctor of any kind. I am just using common sense.

Those who market and promote simulated violence (i.e. video-games) are doing so because of financial gain, and they have no shame about glorifying the contents of their product. It's what the public wants, correct? Absolutely, and because they have high demand for their product, they do everything they can to amplify it to the world. They never decry the violence they depict except when they state, "For mature audiences only." Does anyone even know what a mature audience is? I don't. Is it based on how old you are? Maybe so but the "mature audience" is encouraged to take delight and thrill in simulated brutality. It doesn't take much creativity to capitalize off what they market and promote as cool, sensational, and powerful. Slick marketing and good design skills are put to use in order to tap into people's darkest urges. Why? Because it's attention grabbing and has what I call a "wow" effect. The opposite is much more difficult. Who wants to talk about or initiate programs that promote love, goodness, or doing the right thing? How hard would that be? One certainly must put a lot of thought into providing entertainment that imparts a message of good morals while being fun at the same time.

How do we stop all this violence? It's going to be very difficult because everyone needs to **GIVE A DAMN**: the consumer, the media, politicians, *EVERYONE*. We all have to be on the same page because our success will be dependent upon the weakest link. Consumers need to **GIVE A DAMN** about the kind of entertainment we, and those around us (especially children), choose to watch and participate in. We need to make a conscious decision to stop watching excessively violent movies and not buy our children videogames whose main purpose is to kill as many people as possible. Parents need to limit the use of Ipads, PC play, Internet and phone usage, and instead send their kids out to play. Kick the can, remember that? You never see that anymore. Media outlets need to stop sensationalizing active shooter incidents and better yet, we need to stop watching them altogether. Networks are aware of their viewership and if enough of us tune them out, they will start covering other things (hopefully). If we start to **GIVE A DAMN** and become selective with our media choices, we can change the current landscape of news and entertainment. Everyone needs to **GIVE A DAMN**!

Terrorism

Terrorism is simply an outgrowth of violent crime. It is certainly a topic that has become fixated in our consciousness. ISIS, Al Qaeda, Al Shabaab, and countless other groups have turned into household names, and for the wrong reasons. How to fight the spread of these groups seems to be huge topic in every newspaper, talk show panel, and political debate in the country. No one has a good answer and neither do I. It should never have come to this but it has. I am not here to discuss foreign policy issues, or counter terrorism strategies. These topics are best left to international relations analysts and military experts. But I am here to examine some of the possible root causes of terrorism (many of which are discussed above), and how it relates to the lack of a **GIVE A DAMN** mentality in today's society.

Terrorism is defined as "the use of violence or intimidation in pursuit of political aims." The motives of terrorist groups cover a wide range of subjects: religion, power, land, ideology, and many combinations thereof. Some are desperate, while others seek absolute authority or power. Although the proclaimed goals of terrorist groups are too numerous to list here, the common point is that terrorists use violence and fear in order to coerce a population into doing what they want. They have ceased to **GIVE A DAMN** about the wishes or the well-being of a population (although they will tell you otherwise), and focus only on achieving their self-serving goals through the most ruthless means possible. It's all about them. They become so focused on their ideology that they forget what's really important – the people. All the people; and not just what they might call their "own."

Are terrorists born this way? Absolutely not. As discussed earlier, everyone in the world is born a child, one free from hate or malice. No one ever sees a one or two year old and says, "He is violent," despite thinking of the "terrible two's." Two-year olds are not terrible because they are violent; they are so-called "terrible" because they are exploring, learning, and pushing boundaries. They are innocent and don't know any better. I cannot emphasize this enough. *THEY ARE LEARNING!* And they continue to learn. What they learn today will set the stage for who they will become tomorrow. They learn from parents, society, friends, mentors, schools, everything. As they grow older, their "innocence" is transformed into the adults they become based on all of their childhood experiences.

Time and time again throughout this book I will underline the importance of education. Education from all sources is what shapes young learners into the type of adults they become. Those who receive moral, scholastic, and character based education usually become quality people (like what happens in military schools). They understand right from wrong. They develop traits critical in understanding good behavior and values, and why terrorism is wrong. They understand that the mission of a terrorist is to advance economically or territorially at the expense of others by pushing an extremist ideology. And it's wrong.

Unfortunately in many parts of the world, children grow up in poverty, with no real hope of an education in any sense of the word. They lack both the formal education needed to lift themselves out of poverty, and more importantly the moral teaching to appreciate the value of human life. As a result, they become easy targets for those who wish to exploit their lack of education and turn them into fighters for a cause they barely understand. So they are offered a way out, a way to support something that significantly raises their worth. You can see how easy it would be to take a "down and out" young man with a limited understanding of religion or politics and influence him to fight for a cause. So my guess is that the "terrorist" doesn't really call it terrorism, but rather a fight for a just cause, which in reality is a misguided one. One example is how the Taliban gained influence in Afghanistan. One of the methods they use for radicalizing the population was to only distribute Korans (Islamic sacred book) in Arabic, which the local people did not speak. This meant that they had to rely on distorted translations by Taliban members, which the people were unable to verify for themselves. As a result, the Taliban were able to substitute their own interpretations, as well as position themselves as experts in religion, in order to gain more power over the population.

Although a greater emphasis on formal character education would help solve a large part of this problem, the family and environment also plays an essential role when it comes to how to **GIVE A DAMN**. Often, individuals who become terrorists have unstable or unsupportive family situations. As children, they do not receive the nurturing or moral education that is so important in shaping a healthy adult mind. So in effect, the importance of family life is lost to them. Those who have strong family ties and who are taught the value of how to **GIVE A DAMN** are much less likely to commit violent crimes, let alone become terrorists.

Some, especially those who commit heinous acts, may think terrorists do **GIVE A DAMN** since they will go to any length to achieve their goal. Although this may seem admirable, their thinking has been brain washed, causing them to misunderstand the consequence of their actions and what is right from wrong. Terrorism does not **GIVE A DAMN** about the civilians that are killed in the process. So, what constitutes a terrorist, versus what constitutes a legitimate fighter for a cause? It's not an easy question, and the answer will change depending on the situation. But ultimately, the answer lies in the methods used, and whether the person fighting is driven by external or internal motives. Those who are peacefully motivated to help others outside of themselves and their own ideology are likely to be "right." On the other hand, those who are driven by internal motivation (what's in it for "me") and often includes violence, are probably "wrong", and fighting for the wrong reasons.

Terrorism is a selfish act. So is every crime. These three categories of violent behavior in individuals stem from feeling a lack of control, self esteem, and appreciation; and above all, a lack of hope. Having a **GIVE A DAMN** attitude can help stop violence before it starts. Why? Because it is possible that many perpetrators of violence feel that no one cares about them. If a person was surrounded by **GIVE A DAMN** people, don't you think they would acquire a **GIVE A DAMN** mentality themselves? Don't you think they would feel appreciated? Don't you think society would be a lot better off? While we all have choices, a nurturing **GIVE A DAMN** society can definitely influence people to make positive and correct choices. People will feel better about themselves and others. **GIVE A DAMN** people think about the value of human life above all other things. They also take into consideration the long term consequences of their actions. If we build a society of people who have internalized these two values, we can certainly reduce or stop violence before it starts.

(1) Davey, Monica, and Smith, Mitch. "Murder Rates Rising Sharply in Many U.S Cities." New York Times. 31 August 2015. Web.

(2) http://www.abqjournal.com/345939/opinion/breaking-down-us-murders-by-the-numbers.html. Diane Dimond, Albuquerque Journal, February 1, 2014

(3) http://www.wsj.com/articles/u-s-leads-world-in-mass-shootings-1443905359. Wall Street Journal, October 3, 2015

(4) Towers, Sherry, et al. 2015. *Contagion in Mass Killings and School Shootings.* PLOS-ONE. PLoS ONE 10(7): e0117259. doi:10.1371/journal.pone.0117259

(5) Atkinson, Rowland and Rodgers, Thomas. 2015. *Pleasure Zones and Murder Boxes: Online Pornography and Violent Video Games as Cultural Zones of Exception.* British Journal of Crimonology. 10.1093. 4-17.

CHAPTER 6

Why Should We Care? What Is Our Purpose? Why GIVE A DAMN?

Have you ever wondered about your purpose in life? Why were you born? Why do you exist? Why did God put you on this earth? Can you honestly answer even one of these questions? I have asked hundreds of people these very same questions and most do not have an answer.

I believe that each life is meant to serve a purpose. And that purpose is to serve others, and by serving others we serve ourselves. But people get it reversed. Sometimes it takes a while to figure out what we are meant to do or be in life. Each one of us is destined to follow a different path; but surely our purpose is related to helping others in some way, isn't it? We couldn't have been put on this earth merely to amass wealth. Yet some people think this way. People who are focused on making money are, in general, constantly driven by two thoughts: "What's in it for me?" and, "How can I get ahead?" Honestly, I thought this way for a time and it affected my relationships with family and friends. This pursuit of status and wealth is what sometimes (and overwhelmingly) shapes peoples' life decisions.

My kids sometimes say to me, "Dad, all you think about is money!" I admit that at one point in my life it was probably true, and frankly I suffered the consequences of it. However, it's really only half the story. Most kids don't realize how much money goes into meeting their wants and needs. Providing them with food, shelter, entertainment and a great education (among many other things) isn't free! Once they reach a certain age, they ultimately have to take *full* responsibility for their lives and must fend for themselves.

I worked hard in order to have enough money to provide for my family and my kids, but this was because I wanted them to become independent, responsible adults. When I charged them "rent" for living in my house after they reach their early 20s, they believed that all I thought about was money. What I was really trying to teach them was a continuance of gaining more responsibility as they became adults. But sometimes they did not see it this way. They needed to learn to be on their own (whether in my house or renting an apartment) and to contribute to society. I wanted them to find a means of supporting themselves, even if it was difficult at times for them. I wanted my children to lead purposeful lives, not give them a "free ride!" I wanted them to know that life is not always easy. If this means that all I thought about was money, then so be it, yet I know this is not the case.

So why *did* God put *you* on this earth? As I stated earlier, most people cannot answer this question. It has taken me years to finally realize why I am here. In my eyes it is to serve other people, and make their lives better in whatever way I can (and of course, I am not always good at this but I think my heart is in the right place). And in doing so, I make my own life better. But a lot people don't get this. We serve ourselves by serving others. Isn't that what God wants us to do? Many people don't share this belief because they are focused on serving themselves first. The big question in their minds is: "If I don't look after myself first, who will?" They feel that they must put themselves and their work first in order to provide their families with food and shelter. These are great arguments, but in reality, you are still thinking of your family as being the end result, not yourself. However, you can easily serve others in so many different ways while you are working to support yourself and your family. We can all **GIVE A DAMN** even in small ways, and live a more purposeful and giving life. When we care about others, others will care about us too, at least that's supposed to be how it works. By serving others we serve ourselves; and like I have said before, many have this thought process reversed.

GIVE A DAMN has no religious boundaries. It doesn't matter whether you are Catholic, Protestant, Buddhist, Jewish, Muslim or any other religion. One doesn't even need a religion to incorporate it into their lives. It is a very simple philosophy. You simply invest yourself in caring for others, doing the right thing and being responsible and accountable for your actions. It should be that simple. We do not live in a perfect world and there are things that you simply cannot control, but you do have more control than you might think. Frankly, I don't want to hear about how particular events in someone's life cause him to do bad things or prevent him from doing what's right. We are always finding excuses instead of solutions to problems. These excuses come in a variety of forms, but they all have the same underlying meaning: "It's not my fault." **GIVE A DAMN** people don't view life this way. They don't need to, because taking responsibility for their errors is a source of pride or gratification for them. It's not that **GIVE A DAMN** people never mess up, it's just that they admit it when they do. Plus, there are circumstances in life that you just cannot control (weather as an example) and **GIVE A DAMN** people do not offer excuses for these events that might have caused them harm. They move on and do the best they can. And you know what generally happens: they get help from other **GIVE A DAMN** people!

In every job, you work for money but you also have to serve others in some capacity, which in effect, serves you. Some do this well, others do not. The reason why some serve others poorly is that they don't **GIVE A DAMN**; they work because they *have* to in order to survive. I believe that these people are generally unhappy because they only "think" about serving themselves and their basic needs. They fail to realize that one has to go beyond meeting his or her material needs in order to truly thrive and achieve maximum success. If we went into a work situation with the total desire to help others, our food and shelter would (I believe) be naturally be provided. Most people either don't understand or don't trust this statement, and therefore provide excuses about what cannot be done. Maybe it sounds too good to be true. However, I can assure you from my own experiences, and from the many **GIVE A DAMN** people that I have talked to, it is a fact. Plus, it doesn't cost any money to test this theory for yourself! If you do something wrong, you *will* eventually have to pay for it, monetarily or otherwise, because the truth always wins. You won't lose anything by trying out my **GIVE A DAMN** philosophy, and you could have everything to gain. You should never feel ashamed of doing what is right, especially if it's to the benefit of others as opposed to your own benefit. Why? Because right will always win over wrong, and you will reap the reward. You just might not see it immediately but *it will* happen.

I am a fairly religious person. I pray regularly and also try to go to church every week, primarily to learn something new and to reinforce my beliefs. If you think about it, the Bible is really the closest thing to a **GIVE A DAMN** book. It is not the foundation for this book, but it could be. The Bible does, however, point out (1 Corinthians 10:24), "Nobody should seek his own good but the good of others." Therefore, we should not be conceited, provoking and envious of each other but rather we should be kind and compassionate to one another. Forgiving and understanding translates to someone who **GIVES A DAMN**.

Most have heard the phrase, "You Reap What You Sow." That expression is a good guiding philosophy, but we should never *expect* to reap something in return for what we sow. That is the problem with today's society though. More and more people only do well if they foresee an immediate return or some type of benefit. Otherwise, they are probably very reluctant to do anything at all. We should do things out of the goodness of our hearts by helping others and then leave it in God's hands for the "reap what you sow" reward. God will eventually reward you but you should never expect it.

We need to humble ourselves when dealing with others, and not be misled by our pride. It is written in the Bible, "Whoever exalts himself will be humbled, and he who humbles himself will be exalted." (Matthew 23:12). So never let your ego convince you that you are better or more righteous than another. "Therefore let us stop passing judgment on one another. Instead, make up your mind not to put any stumbling block or obstacle in your brother's way." (Romans 14:13)

To **GIVE A DAMN** means you value and respect others in every way. You value their time, feelings, background, perspective, and preferences (the entire package) even though you might disagree with them on certain issues. Disagreement isn't a bad thing, but a closed mind is. You want to support and help them in any way that you can. Isn't that what excellent customer service is all about in the business world? Yep. Too bad we don't experience more of this in our everyday lives and interactions with other people.

People who **GIVE A DAMN** do not feel like they are somehow above other people, regardless of education, experience, economics status, or any other trait. Successful CEOs treat everyone from the vice president to the janitor as someone of importance. It doesn't matter if you are the head of a major organization or the head of a small retail store. If you **GIVE A DAMN** you will let your esteem for others shine through in your actions. Some people let power and money go to their heads, and think they are above other people. They consider themselves better than those around them, but often spend their lives in fear of losing even a small portion of their worldly possessions and influence. Their wealth gives them outer strength, but they are often weak and afraid on the inside. I am not sure why, but I would suspect it would be in fear of losing it all.

A friend of mine went through a painful divorce after nearly 20 years of marriage. She had married young and had spent most of her adult life raising her children. When her marriage ended, she struggled to find her own identity, separate from that as a wife and mother. She decided to make a career change and eventually felt called to move to another state to pursue another job opportunity. She believed the new job would enable her to make a big difference in the lives of others. To do this, she gave up her house and belongings, took a cut in pay, left her close friends and children (who supported her), and in doing so, made an unbelievable, yet giant leap of faith. She did what few people have the courage to do, especially when it came to her children. She made a plan to make sure she supported and visited them often. She gave up financial security and possessions in the hopes of having a more purpose-driven life. She put her faith in God and trusted that by doing good things for others and her family, good things might be provided to her. With her eyes smiling, she said to me, "I think I know the secret. I have learned that there is little I can do to make myself truly happy. I must depend on God to make me happy and to meet my needs. When I have a need, I have to trust God to supply according to His riches. Most of the time I don't need half of what I think I need, but if I **GIVE A DAMN** and do all that I can for others, He will never let me down. Since I learned that secret, to **GIVE A DAMN**, I am happy." It kind of drives the point home but.....

Can it be that simple? Absolutely. If you reflect on your life, would a bigger house make you happier? You might initially say yes, but in the long term, probably not. Would a better paying job make you happier? Same thought process but probably not. Even if these things did make you happier for a short time, you would eventually want more. That is the nature of material things, there can always be "better." When do you realize your greatest happiness? It is in doing the simple things like sitting on the floor with your kids or grandkids to play games, taking a walk to look at the stars, reading a story for a child or making a meal together...all simple gifts from above. Whether it is an unexpected act of kindness, providing extraordinary customer service, or being sincerely interested in every word that someone says, great **GIVE A DAMN** people usually have one thing in common: they consistently do more than what is expected of them, and do more for others as their primary focus. We were born to **GIVE A DAMN** but way too many people fail to understand what this means, and equally fail to realize how important it really is, in their own life and society as a whole.

Nelson Mandela passed away at the age of 95. He is recognized all over the world as a tremendously influential, life-long advocate for human rights. Although he worked tirelessly for the causes of freedom and empowerment, Nelson Mandela was a servant, and he was proud to be a servant even though suffering greatly in the process. He served others like few people in this world find the strength, stamina and passion to do so. We should all make it our mission in life to find a purpose...to find a means of serving others in big or even small ways. This is what it means to really **GIVE A DAMN**.

There is a song that was often sung at my son's school. The lyrics are as follows:

"Make me a servant, humble and meek.
Lord, let me lift up those who are weak.
And may the prayer of my heart always be,

Make me a servant, make me a servant,
Make me a servant today."

If only we would wake up every morning with these words in mind, and each find a way to be of service to our fellow men and women. I hope that one day people's attitudes will change, and this book is my attempt to contribute to that change. At the end of the day, we are not put on earth for ourselves; we are here for each other, and to serve each other in the best possible way we can. By serving others we serve ourselves. Just don't get it reversed.

CHAPTER 7

What Can Be Done? What Does It Mean to GIVE A DAMN?

No one is perfect. We all can't be Nelson Mandela. Then again, we can certainly try our best to imitate him to some degree. As we grow up, we develop ideas about ourselves and about others, and we also develop habits. These ideas and habits can vary greatly depending on our individual experiences. However, no matter how they are formed and once they are in place, they can be very difficult to change. Ask smokers who want to quit how tough it is. Yet, if you are determined and focused, you *can* and in this case, must change. Perhaps there have been situations in your life where you have thought, "It is okay, because no one will notice what I am about to do." This mentality can range from things as minor as tossing a cigarette out of a car window to major wrongs such as stealing. The overall thought process is that since no one will see you do it, you "justify" it as being okay. We have to stop thinking this way. We all have an inner voice that tells us to do the right thing. We just need to listen to that inner conscience voice, and think about doing more of the *right* things. Once we do them enough, they will become habitual to us on a daily or even hourly basis.

To **GIVE A DAMN** means to take responsibility. Today, many people rarely take responsibility for their actions. When someone makes a mistake it is rare that they will admit they are wrong. It is always someone else's fault, or there is an excuse for what happened because it was beyond their control. We are so quick to blame outside forces (without even thinking about it) for things that we have really brought upon ourselves. We need to live up to our mistakes, admit and correct them, and then move on. I admired the Senator from Louisiana who admitted that he procured services from the infamous "DC Madam Ring." He admitted that what he had done was wrong, even though it surely damaged his reputation, and probably for life. "Fessing up" was the right thing to do. Maybe he made a stupid decision without thinking about right and wrong because he thought he was going to get away with it. He failed to realize that the decision he made back then (wrong as it might be and he probably knew it) would have repercussions tomorrow. And it did. What you do wrong (lie, steal, cheat, etc.) will *always* come out sooner or later. Always.

No matter how difficult your life is or how bad a situation might be, you should always take responsibility for your actions. And it can actually be good for you. For instance, a 23 year-old daughter of one of my friends was in a car accident several years ago. She had graduated with honors from college and just gotten a full scholarship to law school. She had everything going for her. She worked at a restaurant and went home late at night after having a few beers. While driving, she received a text message, and as she glanced down, the car in front of her braked suddenly. She swerved, but still rear ended the other car, causing much more damage to her own vehicle than the one she hit. When she got out of the car she realized what she had done and the potential effect it could have had on the rest of her life. She was quite scared and was completely honest with the other driver. She told him she had been looking at her phone and hit him by accident. She said she would take full responsibility for what happened and pay for the damage. The police arrived soon after the other driver called. Again she was honest and told the policeman the same thing. The police officer was very cordial and understanding. Even though she had been drinking (but under the limit and willing to take a breathalyzer test) and texting when she shouldn't have, the officer said, "Thank you for your honesty. It's really rare these days. I am not going to give you a ticket, just be more careful. I think you learned a lesson." She did the right thing, despite her fear of repercussion, which could have been much more severe. Two **GIVE A DAMN** people in the same instance. One took responsibility and the other was compassionate and rewarded her for it. She was very lucky because she could have lost her full scholarship, been arrested for drunk driving (although she was under the limit), lost her license for 6 months and might have had to perform several hours of community service. Or worse yet, she could have caused personal injury to another human being. **GIVE A DAMN** people don't blame others or outside circumstances, and more times than not they will be rewarded because they admitted their mistake, took responsibility for it and then fixed it. The truth always wins.

When we make a decision, we need to understand the consequences of making that decision and suffer and accept the consequences no matter how severe the potential penalty. It doesn't matter what effect it might have on you or for how long, what matters most is that you understand the pros and cons of your decision and take responsibility for it. You do it when you invest in stocks, right? For example, if you lose money based on a broker's recommendation, should you sue your broker because he recommended it? No, you take the information, analyze the facts and make a decision. Now, if the broker provided you with fraudulent information, then you can take the appropriate action.

Princess Diana of Great Britain, who died tragically in 1997 said, "Carry out a random act of kindness, with no expectation of reward, safe in the knowledge that one day someone might do the same for you." It is such a great statement! It's amazing what the power of kindness can do. Kindness allows us to connect to hearts, touch souls, and transform lives. In addition to the effect that our kindness has on others, kindness is great for our own health. There have been multiple scientific studies that emphasize this fact. Adult altruism can be defined as acts of "voluntary behavior that is motivated by concern for the welfare of others, rather than by the anticipation of rewards." Sound familiar? Of course it does since you have gotten this far in the book. Many studies have found that people, especially the elderly, who perform acts of altruism have more of a will to live, have increased life satisfaction, and a greater overall well-being than those who do not; and as a result, they live longer (1). Another study by the University of California at Berkeley has shown that older people who participated in volunteerism had a 44% lower likelihood of dying during the study period than those who did not (2). We often focus on the benefits of eating healthy and exercising, but the health benefits of simple kindness are just as significant! Did you know that? **GIVE A DAMN** people who act with kindness and bring goodness into the lives of others live longer!! Don't we all want that?

Words that we speak along with our actions are very powerful; they can either build others up or tear them down. Language choice not only makes a difference in how our listeners feel, but how we perceive the situation as well. For example, would you rather wear a jacket that is "old" or "vintage"? What about a neighbor who is "eccentric" versus one who is "crazy"? These words can be used to describe the exact same thing, but our outlook changes immensely based on which ones we use. The same is true with our actions when combined with words. For example, I can tell you that "I love you" in a soft and caring manner, or I can tell you "I love you" in a fearful tone of voice with my hands getting ready to be clenched around your neck. The point being, our tone of voice along with our actions has a lot to do with how our words come across. In fact, tone of voice can sometimes be more important than the words that are actually spoken. We need to watch what we say and be careful in how we use our words, along with how we act when delivering our words. We can always get our point across in a positive and caring way, if we just put some thought into it before actually speaking. I know, it's a lot easier said than done, but we can all do it!

GIVE A DAMN boils down to how we think, and how that thinking translates into our behavior. We have to maintain a positive attitude and not feel that others are out to get us. We cannot become bitter when we can't control everything that happens around us. We cannot be jealous because someone put in hard work and became wealthy (of course luck could be involved, too, but most people create their own luck). They earned it. And, we cannot always win every time either.

Most of us can come up with a list of people who have demonstrated through their actions that they did **GIVE A DAMN** and others who did not. The following sign was taken off the inside door of a men's bathroom where I used to work. For months, someone kept throwing paper towels on the floor after drying his hands, despite the fact that the waste basket was only four feet away from the exit door. Eventually, the cleaning lady got fed up and placed a sign on the door that read:

"This is intended for the individual who keeps dropping paper towels on the floor here at the door. I assume you are drying your hands with the towels and in some extreme, fastidious sense of cleanliness, you hope to avoid germs by opening the door using the towel as a shield. Then you simply drop the towel on the floor as you leave. Good move, but a selfish act, since somebody has to come along behind you and pick up your soiled towel. Please, in the future, simply open the door using the towel as you have in the past, but take the towel with you and drop it in the trash can in your office."

Would this person do the same thing in his own house? Probably not!

Let me offer you a suggestion: begin to observe people and see which ones perform actions that show they **GIVE A DAMN**. They are not greedy or self-centered. They lead by example. They are humble, and let their actions speak for themselves. They are servants. They work with people, for people, and they don't feel like anything is beneath them. They are team players. They do things that are right, even though it might be to their detriment. They listen to their conscience. **GIVE A DAMN** people are leaders who want to help others, even if it means putting in the extra work. It's just the right thing to do. If you know how to **GIVE A DAMN**, leaders will come to you for help, which now makes you a *leader* as well!

Even in a bad situation, you can always find good. You just have to think about it from a different angle. A friend of mine had a teenage son who was an outstanding athlete and a straight "A" student at a prestigious university. After a night out drinking with friends, he got in his car to drive home, despite the fact that he was too drunk to be behind the wheel. He got in a one-car accident and tragically died. Now there is absolutely nothing positive about this incident, right? Probably from one angle, yes. But, when you put this tragic incident in a different perspective, maybe there is. I must emphatically point out that by no means am I suggesting this tragic event was good in any way. Far from it. Yet, this young man saved two lives by donating his organs to people who would have died without them. Even more importantly, the hundreds of his teenage friends who attended his funeral learned a valuable lesson: drinking and driving don't mix. This young man's friends saw first-hand the deadly consequences of drunk driving. Therefore, they now know better than to get in a car with someone who has been drinking, let alone drive intoxicated themselves. So, as difficult as this may sound, on the positive side such a tragic accident might save the lives of others from a similar fate. By focusing on the positive, more and more people will actually **GIVE A DAMN** because they are thinking not only on the immediate effects a situation has on them, but how it affects others as well.

I read an article in 2008 about employees of a major city who had city credit cards and racked up exorbitant lunch charges. Now mind you, these cards were the financial responsibility of the city. Although one would expect the city to cover reasonable meal expenses for business or lobbying meetings, one charge for lunch was over $3,800. Now, I don't know the logistics behind these charges but it would appear to me that this lunch bill was excessively high. It brought to mind this question: Do you think that these employees would have racked up the same charges if they were paying out of their own pocket? I doubt it. Your mindset is usually different when you are paying with someone else's (like a company's) money. When it doesn't affect you, your **GIVE A DAMN** barometer goes way down. Why? Because your mindset might shift to one of entitlement, causing you to think something along the lines of, "the city can afford it and I deserve it because of all the hard work I do." But what if you had to foot the entire bill yourself? Would your thinking change? Of course it would! We should all spend other people's money like it's our own (despite the fact that someone or some organization has wealth). Do you? If you do, then you **GIVE A DAMN**.

As I have stated before, people should be more concerned about what they can put into a situation rather than what they can get out of it. Too many people think in reverse (whether they know it or not) by thinking (and probably subconsciously), "What's in it for me?" **GIVE A DAMN** thinking isn't like that: you think about others and what is best for them, not for yourself. What people don't realize is that in almost every case, you will get something out of it, but you should never expect it. In most instances you will (or should) at least get a simple thank you. This simple gesture needs to provide you with the satisfaction that you have helped someone.

GIVE A DAMN people know how to collaborate. Collaborative people are team players, colleagues, helpers, partners, co-workers, compatriots and more. There is never an occasion in which they ask themselves, "What's in it for me," because that's not their primary goal. The "for me" attitude is not associated with **GIVE A DAMN** people because they know something good will come out of it in the end. You win when everyone else wins, but people just don't understand or truly believe in this philosophy.

One of the many things **GIVE A DAMN** people seem to have in common is an appreciation for achievement – their own and that of others. They focus on the team being successful, because then everybody wins. They understand that accomplishments are one of the best ways to motivate people, including themselves and their coworkers. Success is something to be enjoyed, celebrated, and encouraged. **GIVE A DAMN** people are cheerleaders for positive contributions.

Have you ever thought about offering a smile to everyone you meet, whether you know them or not? I conducted a non-scientific experiment on this. I looked at people in total disgust and then I also looked at people by smiling. Do you realize the reactions I got when I looked at someone in disgust? Whoa! I could not believe it. Everyone looked at me like I was jerk (there is another word for it, actually). The ones to whom I smiled, smiled back, even if sometimes I could detect a level of pain in their expressions. It just was the right thing to do.

Far too many of us think we **GIVE A DAMN** when we actually don't. We all slip sometimes. It takes time and constant attention to change our mindset, but it is important to make the effort. **GIVE A DAMN** thinking must take precedent over any and all of our actions. We all have a little voice inside of us, whispering to do the right thing. All we have to do is listen to it. Over many years you may have been guided by negative influences but don't let these influences stop you from thinking about how you can **GIVE A DAMN**. You know the truth, so act upon it properly, as painful or difficult as it might be. Egocentricity can and will destroy, if not kill, you.

When someone does something nice for you, how do you feel? Not only does it make you feel good but the person providing the act of kindness feels good, too. You both smile. Now what about the opposite? If someone is rude or mean to you, how do you feel? You are perhaps surprised, amazed, upset or confused, but in all cases it doesn't feel good. I can assure you the rude person isn't feeling too well either. So conflict is now created, and if not handled properly it can result in something much worse. So, smile more often (like right now). It does a body good. Too often we underestimate the power of a touch, a smile, a kind word, a listening ear, an honest compliment, or the smallest act of caring, all of which have the potential to turn a life around. And guess what? Such acts help us live longer!

I also think part of the problem is that people are just oblivious to their surroundings. It's a condition of not thinking about the effect their actions might have on people around them, or for that matter, the effect their actions might have on people that come *after* them. It's a classic case of "out of sight, out of mind." For example, men urinating in the toilet when the seat is down. There is a really good chance that a man's aim won't be perfect, and if you are perfect, there is an even better chance the water might just splash up on the seat when it is flushed. How would you feel if you came behind someone who had just urinated, sat down and the seat was wet? Public restrooms are the worst! It feels like it's all over you. It has happened to everyone, male and female. Talk about a sickening feeling and being a little pissed off (no pun intended). It was because the person before you didn't **GIVE A DAMN** about how his action (or lack of action) might have affected you or anybody else, after what he had done. For goodness sake…. put the seat up.

Once, there was a guy washing windows in a building I was in. He had just washed two windows directly above the glass door going in and out of the building. When the door opened up, I noticed a pool of water on the tile floor. This was a ticket for disaster. People exiting the building might not notice the water. Therefore, the possibility of someone slipping was extremely high. As I was leaving I had to gingerly walk through the water for fear of slipping myself (there was no way around it either, so you had to walk through it). The washer had no concern about the water on the floor that could cause someone to slip and get hurt. He hadn't even bothered to put up a "WET FLOOR" sign. The probability of someone slipping and falling was very high and if this had happened, the cleaning company could have been sued (and unless our litigious society changes, it is highly likely that would have been the case).

Now, let's think a little differently. If this same person was washing windows over the front door and his 85 year-old father came out with the pool of the water on the floor, what do you think he would have done? **DAMN** right, he would have made sure the water was gone so his father would not slip and fall. We have to think about how our actions might affect others, no matter who they are. So I asked the window washer if he had a towel so that I could wipe up the floor so no one would slip coming in or out of the building. He became a bit flustered and stated, "I'll get it," and he immediately cleaned up the water. I was a bit confused and thought, "I guess he was oblivious to what he was doing or just did not **GIVE A DAMN**."

I personally think a lot of people simply don't know how to **GIVE A DAMN**. But others instinctively know how, because of how they were raised, the role models involved in their life or from watching others in their community. I believe this is called "common courtesy," the sister of "common sense." It is a caring and respectful attitude you have for one another. When you were growing up, think of the many people that helped you with schoolwork, your career, or other personal situations. We have all had these people in our lives, since no one can get through life completely on his own. Most knew how to **GIVE A DAMN** and expected nothing in return. The people we associate with and our role models in life (including our parents) are so important in the person that we eventually become.

When you **GIVE A DAMN**, *you do the right thing.* Think about it. Everyone should know how to distinguish between right and wrong. We just have to listen to our mind and heart. We need to stop and ask ourselves, "What is the right thing to do?" We will always get the answer, maybe not an answer we would like, but in the greater scheme of things it is the right one. Choosing to do the right thing is not always easy. But by doing it over and over again, it eventually becomes a part of you.

A priest and good friend of mine sent me an email that said, "Never underestimate the power of being nice to someone." It means you **GIVE A DAMN**. The danger is in believing that being nice to someone will get you something in return. Then it becomes a self-serving behavior, because you expect something in return for what you did. This also does not mean you should allow a person to take advantage of you because you know how to **GIVE A DAMN** and the other person does not. If another person doesn't **GIVE A DAMN** over and over again, the best remedy is to avoid him.

It is important to allow others to share their ideas with you even if their ideas conflict with yours. Before getting defensive about seemingly critical comments (especially if they are directed at you), pause to listen and consider. Many times when people say something to or about us that is perceived to be critical we immediately become defensive. We think about what the person has said and how he said it, but we don't always think about the reason for the comment. In many situations, criticism from others can be constructive, if we remain open to it. Criticism from others should be viewed as an opportunity for self-improvement. In most situations, there is some element of truth in what has been said (although delivered in a bad way); we just don't want to admit it. If you listen intently to *what* is being said and not the *way* it is being said (which can put you on the defensive), you might be able to find something in which you can improve upon. It is best to offer constructive criticism to others *only* when your feedback has been solicited. And then, the key is to offer comments in a way that shows you **GIVE A DAMN** about the other person. For instance, approaching an overweight stranger and pointing out that he should really lose some weight, is not likely to go over well, even if it is the truth. A comment like this from a stranger is likely to hurt feelings and it shows a lack of sensitivity.

During a business trip, I found myself on a flight that had been completely booked, with only three single seats available and scattered throughout the plane. A mother and her two small children were the last ones to board. As a result, all three had to sit in separate seats. The attendant asked if there were three people in a row who would be willing to move so the family could sit together. One row agreed. They got up and went to separate seats. I watched the mother, and not once did she ever say thank you to any of them. Maybe she was busy with her kids, but really, she should have at least made some effort to acknowledge the kindness of three total strangers. Perhaps this mother never thought about her kids being split up and how traumatic that might have been for them. These three strangers surely understood the situation and demonstrated how to **GIVE A DAMN**. In so doing, they made one mother's life a whole lot better for that plane ride. I just did not understand her lack of appreciation.

When someone does something nice for you or gives you a gift or compliment, you should thank him and do it in a special way. This is what I call the Attitude of Gratitude! It really should not matter on the size of the nice thing that was done for you. Our society underestimates the power of the simple words "Please," "Thank you" and even "Excuse me." It is amazing to me how many people never say these words anymore. Thank you letters and personal notes are becoming a lost art because of the Internet. Most of us now communicate appreciation (if we do it at all) through email or text messages (because it is easy and fast). This is better than nothing, but not as meaningful as a hand-written note. In an effort to address this situation, there are now special thank you messages that can be sent through video email. A video message is recorded and then emailed to the person. Also, online greeting cards can now be created and emailed to thank someone for a good deed. This seems to be the way that thank you notes will be sent in the future, but kids still need to be taught the Attitude of Gratitude at an early age. It shows you care and that you **GIVE A DAMN** by thanking others for their kindness.

If you really want to **GIVE A DAMN**, you are going to need energy, compassion and self-awareness to make it work. You will be amazed at the positive effect it will have on people. This is not something that can be done overnight. It might be difficult to do at first, especially as an adult, but you have to start somewhere. It should start at home and at the earliest age possible. You must take responsibility for your own actions and show that you can and will **GIVE A DAMN** in everything that you say and do. It will rub off on others, especially your children. It's so important for this world and we have to do it one person at a time. Some years ago, I volunteered to chair a $4 million dollar capital campaign to help raise funds for the renovation of my children's church and school. What could I possibly get out of this? Nothing directly, but that wasn't the point. I wanted my kids to have the best education possible and I knew I would meet a lot of nice, giving people along the way and make new friends.

When you do something, it will affect both you and others. This is always the case, because we do not operate in a vacuum. Your thinking should be based on the effect your actions or words will have on others. You set the tone with a **GIVE A DAMN** attitude. The effect of whatever you do might not be immediate but it will certainly have an impact on you at some point in the future. When we think about all of the people who clearly **GIVE A DAMN** and those who seemingly do not (and many are skewed to the "do not" group), it always boils down to one behavior: thinking about the consequences of our actions on others, whether in the present or future. Too many people just think about the job they have to do, or think of how things might affect them personally. Society has simply become self-centered, thereby ignoring other people. Over a period of time, this causes tension (and violence) and it grows like a cancer. When it comes to helping people in a disaster, people are more than willing to help. We become compassionate and understanding and we reach out because we think about how we would feel if such a thing were to happen to us. We relate. But sadly, once the catastrophe disappears from the media, it often disappears from people's minds and thoughts as well. How great would it be if we all behaved with this generosity and compassion every day? And it became a habit and not an exception? It would be terrific!

(1) http://www.stonybrook.edu/bioethics/goodtobegood.pdf; August 2009, by Stephen G. Post, PhD; professor and director, Center for Medical Humanities, Compassionate Care, and Bioethics, Stony Brook University, Stony Brook, N.Y.
(2) Pacific Marine Credit Union, November, 2014. https://www.pmcu.com/?Cabinet=Main&Drawer=Resources&Folder=Education+Center&SubFolder=The+Greatest+Gift

CHAPTER 8

Start A Revolution! How Do We Begin To GIVE A DAMN?

B ecause you have persisted in reading this book, you now understand our problems and hopefully agree with most of my assertions. *You* want to help change society for the better, one person at a time. This chapter continues to review a number of points already touched upon, and which I would like to emphasize further.

When I state, "start a revolution," I mean it in a positive way. It's a movement in a positive direction and it starts with you! It won't be easy but if you think about it, it won't be that hard, either. After all, becoming more conscious and caring about other people is not something that requires any amount of money, physical strength, or talent. It starts as a thought process that becomes ingrained in your brain every minute of every day, and then it "becomes you." It is something everyone is capable of doing. We just need more and more people committed to **GIVING A DAMN** every day, one small deed and one thought at a time, and then together we can start a **GIVE A DAMN** revolution.

It begins with passion and energy. With passion and energy, we can make just about anything happen. When we are passionate about something, we think about it all of the time and then it becomes part of our psyche. It is what we want more than anything in the world, and we will go to great lengths to make it happen. You see this type of passion in athletes who are driven to succeed, in dedicated teachers, in prosperous entrepreneurs, and all other successful people, regardless of their field. Do you need to be passionate in order to **GIVE A DAMN**? It helps. Passion provides the motivation to really make a difference. We also need to get back to basics. And it starts with awareness.

I think a lot of people don't **GIVE A DAMN** because they just don't know any better. They are unaware of their surroundings and how their actions might affect others. People don't realize the consequences of their actions, but it may not be entirely their fault. People are brought up in multiple environments that just don't teach how to **GIVE A DAMN**. If you don't understand the things you should and should not do, how can you change? It is a problem within our changing society that stems from our cultural environment and our education system. There is just not enough focus on what it takes to be a quality human being, or the message is certainly not getting across.

Sometimes it's not easy to tell what is the right or wrong thing to do. Let me explain by giving you an example. You come to a stop sign while driving and a pedestrian is ready to cross the street. You allow him to cross, but he walks slowly instead of hurrying so that you might get on your way. There is no clear-cut distinction between right and wrong in this example. The man just did not care enough about the value of your time, even if it was only for a few seconds. People that **GIVE A DAMN** value other people's time. They hurry across the street when a car stops for them. This is the considerate thing to do. Don't you think the person in the car appreciates it? The **GIVE A DAMN** person in the car then waves, to indicate that he appreciates the effort. And that too, makes a difference to the pedestrian.

Awareness is the first step towards developing a **GIVE A DAMN** mentality. As stated in Chapter 7, you should become aware of the people around you and notice those who do and do not **GIVE A DAMN**. When making your observations, ask yourself these questions: what is the ratio of people around you who do and do not **GIVE A DAMN**? In which situations are **GIVE A DAMN** attitudes common, and in which are they lacking? What can you do to improve this ratio? As a result of observing others, you will become more aware of your own actions and words in certain circumstances. You will then start asking yourself, "Did I **GIVE A DAMN**?" Slowly but surely (and over time) it will become a natural process. You will start to **GIVE A DAMN** as your awareness of your own and other's actions increase. Start making mental notes of those who do and do not **GIVE A DAMN**. You don't have to write it down (although it would be more effective if you did), but be aware of it. Do this for a whole week and see what you come up with. When you look back on past events of that week, you will begin to ask: Did I **GIVE A DAMN**? Soon, you will be able to analyze your actions before they occur, and bring them up to a **GIVE A DAMN** standard.

Observing others and how they behave is the best way to learn how to **GIVE A DAMN**. This works in both directions. When you observe someone who does **GIVE A DAMN**, you begin to internalize what actions really count. When you observe someone who doesn't, it helps underline how negative their actions are, and you can better judge what is right and wrong! At the same time, we need to be aware of our own thinking process, biases, and some of the insecurities and fears that impede our progress. For most of us, this will mean making some conscious changes. Ideally, we should teach our children to consider these things at an early age. This type of self-examination and reflection is important for people of all ages and can lead to very positive results. **GIVE A DAMN** can be translated into caring about what other people want and need more than what you want and need. Of course, you cannot help people all of the time, and there will be people who will try to take advantage of you; but putting the needs of others above your own is always a good motto to live by.

So now that you have become more aware, what do you do next? You turn this awareness into action, and start implementing a **GIVE A DAMN** attitude into your everyday life. When you **GIVE A DAMN**, it has to become personal. One of the most important things we can do as individuals is to see others the same way that we see those we love. Think about it. Don't you **GIVE A DAMN** for those you love? Why can't you do this at some level with others? We need to see other people as we see those who we love, perhaps not to the same degree, but it needs to happen, nonetheless. We need to work towards treating people we don't know (including those from different economic, racial and religious backgrounds) with respect and dignity.

The Bible says in Mark 12:31, "You shall love your neighbor as yourself," but it does not mean just your next-door neighbor. You need to think about how your actions might affect everyone; no matter who or where they are, where they are from, and more importantly, no matter how far into the future these effects might reach. For instance, that rusty nail left in the road could be driven over by someone and get lodged in her tire. Because this could potentially happen to anyone, you pick up the rusty nail and throw it away. We need to continually think this way and be aware of the effect that we have on our surroundings at all times.

Nobody is perfect, but as the saying goes, "It's better to aim for perfection and miss, than to aim for imperfection and hit it." You are going to make mistakes, so if you make a mistake, admit it, apologize, and then take responsibility to fix the mistake. People really don't expect you to be perfect, but most expect you to be honest (you would think). Often, we subconsciously want others to **GIVE A DAMN** about us; yet when it comes to our own thoughts and actions, we don't **GIVE A DAMN** because we are too wrapped up in a self-serving attitude. People want others to think of them, but at the same time, they think about themselves more than others without even realizing it. Mathew 7:12 states, "Do unto others as you would have others do unto you." This applies to people who **GIVE A DAMN**. So when you make a mistake, no matter how trivial, admit it. Whatever you do, don't try to find a way to justify the mistake by blaming someone or something that happened.

Although we can never be perfect, how we frame our imperfections in our minds is what shapes our feelings about them. Think about it. Different ways of framing a situation can either discourage us from continuing, or encourage us to persist and do better. It all depends on whether our thinking is positive or negative. Here is an anecdote to illustrate this point. A 13 year old just started playing golf and became passionate about the game. He practiced every day, and he got better and better. He started shooting in the 90's, then the mid 80's and then the low 80's and then one day shot a 75. Instead of seeing that he was getting better and better, he complained that he was one under par after 12 holes but then had several bogeys in a row that "ruined" his score. He wound up shooting a 3 over par 75 and he was upset. He was down on himself for missing a few opportunities, not realizing that he had his best score ever. Instead of building on this accomplishment, he dwells on a few bad holes. It is good to keep striving to be the best you can be but not at the expense of negative thinking. Case in point: Another newbie golfer keeps getting 7's and 8's on holes but then gets a couple of pars and shoots a 105. His thought was, "Wow, I had two great pars on the back nine and that is something I can build on the next time I play." It is a difference in mindsets that can change our perception of our abilities, environment, and deeds, and also how we react to them.

If you're like most, chances are you've had to work with a person with a "bad attitude" — people who are not committed to their work, their customers, or other team members. They're toxic and a drain on you and everybody else around them. It's not exactly fun working with them is it? On the other hand, you've also likely worked with people who have positive energy and radiate this to everyone around them. Those with a positive attitude not only help get things done, but they make the workplace more satisfying for others. They create a synergy and energy that enhances the entire team. With few exceptions, everyone wants to work with people who do things cooperatively, enthusiastically, and with a minimum of problems. You need that from others and they need it from you. So, what are you doing to make that work? Are you a contributor or are you getting in the way? Exactly what are you doing to build commitment and positive attitudes? Boosting your commitment and attitude, as well as that of others, is a challenge that requires you to invest time, attention, and effort. But it's worth the investment and everyone will reap the benefits of an engaging work environment that produces more rewards for all, including you!

A common theme in many of the presentations I have given in the past, and something I often remind employees of my company and other companies as a business coach and consultant is this: "I don't care about revenue." "What? Are you are crazy?" That's what you're thinking, right? You see, I care most about providing the best customer service possible. Some CEOs would probably disagree with my motto of, "Customer service is what counts, not revenue." They would probably insist that revenue is the most important component of any business. I agree with this actually, but in a lot of cases I think they have it backwards. It is customer service and quality of care that drives revenue, not vice versa. If you provide the absolutely best quality and customer service, the revenue will follow, and more so than you might think. That is one of the success factors of **GIVE A DAMN**. If you give more to someone than what they expect, they will want to do business with you over and over again. This doesn't mean you have to provide more products, it means providing more attention, more service, and more follow up with customers. In business, it's often the little touches that count the most. It is not about revenue, it's about how to **GIVE A DAMN**. If you **GIVE A DAMN**, the revenue will come. Too many people think about the end result, rather than the actions that get you there; the added personal touches, the extra service and support and the value add that really drives revenue. It costs nothing and can improve everything around you and the organization.

Every member of an organization should have the same **GIVE A DAMN** attitude, whether he is the President or part of a custodial staff. Each is just as important as the other and just because you have a title does not mean you are entitled. There are many executives who refuse to do tasks that they feel are beneath them because they fear it will affect their status. In fact, it's a matter of their egos getting in the way, not their status. What do you think this says about them? It shows they are not team players and feel they are better than others. Who wants to do business with these kind of people? Simple gestures such as returning an email, getting a drink for someone, or not keeping a person waiting for an appointment are important **GIVE A DAMN** examples of what the president of a corporation should do, regardless of the size of the organization. This **GIVE A DAMN** attitude will then translate to other employees, causing the company to become much more successful.

GIVE A DAMN people also have a sense of urgency. They are attuned to helping people and doing it quickly. They don't procrastinate. They get things done. One difference between good and bad customer service is a sense of urgency; or more importantly people who **GIVE A DAMN**. A sense of urgency means you want to get something done without delay, and it is the right thing to do. Those who act quickly, efficiently, and effectively are as successful in business as they are in their personal lives.

The point is that when you **GIVE A DAMN** you create positive personal relationships with people. If a person **GIVES A DAMN**, there is a ripple effect, and everyone wins. Other people will have a positive opinion about you and your organization, and they will strive to follow your example. Personal relationships are the fruit of the soul from which all successes begin and end. **GIVE A DAMN** is your path to advancement and achievement in all areas as depicted in the following Success Graph:

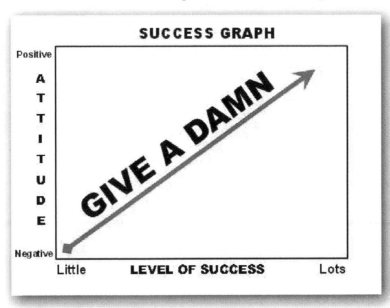

We can start a **GIVE A DAMN** revolution through even the smallest acts of kindness. Each act will reverberate through society, eventually causing the overall thought process to change among people. Those who are the beneficiaries of good deeds usually go on to perform good deeds of their own. People, especially those who are younger, tend to imitate what they see others do. If a **GIVE A DAMN** attitude seeps into the culture at large, even the most resistant to this way of thinking will begin to change their ways, simply in order to fit in with the rest of society, or they will leave! This sounds easy but it's a process that will take time. It's worth the effort though! **"Individually we make a difference, collectively we change the world."**

Five Important GIVE A DAMN Lessons

1) The Janitor – A university professor gave a pop science quiz. All of the questions were right from the textbook and lectures until the last question: "What is the first name of the janitor who cleans this building?" Surely this was a joke, right? Everyone had seen the old man, but how would they know his name? One of the students handed in his paper, leaving the last question blank. When the class ended, a student asked if the last question would count toward the quiz. "Absolutely," said the professor. "In your careers, you will meet many people. All are significant. They deserve your attention and care, even if all you do is smile and say, hello." **Lesson: GIVE A DAMN people value other people no matter who they are.**

2) Pickup in the Rain – One night, at 11:30 PM, an older African American woman was standing on the side of an Alabama highway, trying to endure a huge rain storm. Her car had broken down and she desperately needed a ride. Soaking wet, she decided to flag down the next car. A young white man stopped to help her, generally unheard of in the conflict-filled 1960's. The man took her to safety, helped her get assistance and put her into a taxicab. She seemed to be in a big hurry, but wrote down his address and thanked him. Seven days went by and a knock came on the man's door. To his surprise, a giant console color TV was delivered to his home. A special note was attached. It read, "Thank you so much for assisting me on the highway the other night. The rain drenched not only my clothes, but also my spirits. Then you came along. Because of you, I was able to make it to my dying husband's bedside just before he passed away...God Bless you for helping me and unselfishly serving others." Sincerely, Mrs. Nat King Cole. **Lesson: GIVE A DAMN people always get rewarded sooner or later, they just don't expect it.**

3) Remember Those Who Serve – A 10-year-old boy entered a hotel coffee shop and sat at a table. A waitress put a glass of water in front of him. "How much is an ice cream sundae?" he asked.

"Fifty cents," replied the waitress. The little boy pulled his hand out of his pocket and studied the coins in it. "Well, how much is a plain dish of ice cream?" he inquired. By now more people were waiting for a table and the waitress was growing impatient. "Thirty-five cents," she brusquely replied. The little boy again counted his coins. "I'll have the plain ice cream," he said. The waitress brought the ice cream, put the bill on the table and walked away. The boy finished the ice cream, paid the cashier, and left. When the waitress came back, she began to cry as she wiped down the table. There, placed neatly beside the empty dish, were two nickels and five pennies. You see, he couldn't have the sundae, because he had to have enough left to leave her a tip. **Lesson: GIVE A DAMN people do the right thing.**

4) Obstacles in Our Path. In ancient times, a King had a boulder placed on a roadway. Then he hid himself and watched to see if anyone would remove the huge rock. Some of the King's wealthiest merchants and courtiers came by and simply walked around it. Many loudly blamed the King for not keeping the roads clear, but none did anything about getting the stone out of the way. Then a peasant came along, carrying a load of vegetables. Upon approaching the boulder, the peasant laid down his burden and tried to move the stone to the side of the road. After much pushing and straining, he finally succeeded. After the peasant picked up his load of vegetables, he noticed a purse lying in the road where the boulder had been. The purse contained many gold coins and a note from the King indicating that the gold was for the person who removed the boulder from the roadway. The peasant learned what many of us never understand. **Lesson: Obstacles present GIVE A DAMN opportunities to help others and by doing so we help ourselves.**

5) Giving When it Counts – Years ago, a friend worked as a volunteer at a hospital and got to know a little girl named Callie, who was suffering from a rare and serious disease. Her only chance of recovery appeared to be a blood transfusion from her 5 year-old brother Jim, who had miraculously survived the same disease and had developed the antibodies needed to combat the illness. The doctor explained the situation to Jim, and asked him if he would be willing to give his blood to his sister. He hesitated only for only a moment before taking a deep breath and saying, "Yes I'll do it, if it will save her." As the transfusion progressed, he lay in bed next to Callie and smiled, as we all did, seeing the color returning to her cheeks. Then Jim's face grew pale and his smile faded. He looked up at the doctor and asked with a trembling voice, "Will I start to die right away?" Being so young, Jim had misunderstood the doctor; he thought he was going to have to give his sister all of his blood in order to save her. **Lesson: GIVE A DAMN people always think about others before themselves**

Each of us has the ability to choose. You can change your thoughts and behaviors if you so wish. It is *imperative* to listen to what your mind and heart is telling you, so that you can make the best decisions in order to do the most good. You cannot change anyone directly but you can change yourself. I believe everyone in life has, for the most part, good intentions. But most people, unless fully committed, will not put **GIVE A DAMN** intentions into action. The reason is that we have learned behavior over many years that is hard to change and frankly so are our habits. It's like trying to quit smoking. Ask anyone who has tried, and they will tell you it's really tough. You have to really want it (this is where passion and motivation come into play). I am a firm believer that if you want something badly enough, you will go to great lengths and sacrifices to make it happen. And I am quite sure you can think of a circumstance in the past where you have had the energy and passion to obtain something that was vastly important to you. And you were successful! If you feel you cannot do it on your own, ask God for help, or enlist a loved one to support you in your efforts. At the end of the day, you will feel terrific. There is nothing better in the world than helping someone in need, especially if it's someone who cannot help himself.

You will learn to **GIVE A DAMN** by doing. Don't get discouraged if it takes longer than what you initially expect, you are not going to change your behavior overnight. Old habits die hard. But it is so important that you go for it, confident that you *will* succeed. One person at a time and it begins with you. **GIVE A DAMN** needs to become your new way of thinking and doing over time. When you encounter a difficult situation or feel yourself slipping, repeat to yourself, I **GIVE A DAMN**, I **GIVE A DAMN**," and over time you will get it. Write it down on a piece of paper and stick it on a mirror or door so that you will see a visual reminder every day. Wear our **GIVE A DAMN** wristband as a constant reminder. Tell others you are a **GIVE A DAMN** person. Tell others to join you. Show them your wristband. This phrase will then become engrained in your psyche and you will notice a gradual change in your attitude and in your interactions with others. As your habits change, your actions will start to rub off on other people and they too will start to **GIVE A DAMN**. And you'll be happier. We need to work on this one person and one incident at a time. It will take time but all good things do. Commit and then just do it!

I am going to repeat this because I think it is important. I believe Mom or a significant mentor is perhaps the strongest motivator to making sure you always **GIVE A DAMN**. You have to assume that your mother (or someone vastly important to you) is always watching everything you say, think and do. Who wants to disappoint Mom? If you think your mother is watching, you will most likely do the right thing, correct? In actuality though, isn't your maker always watching you? There are people who don't think this way because they don't believe in God, but everyone has had, or does have a Mom or role model figure. If this is what it takes for you to **GIVE A DAMN**, I am all for it.

It is not about what society can do for you, it's about what you can do for society and your fellow human beings. How much clearer can this get? The more you do for society, the more you will get in return. And yes, there will be times when you derive no obvious benefit from your good actions. However, when all is said and done, both society and your ultimate maker will reward you. It's just the right thing to do!

I am going to get a bit religious because I believe it drives home a point. But, if you are not at all religious, skip reading the rest of this paragraph and go to the next chapter. Always thank God for His goodness. Anytime something good happens, big or little, give God thanks. "Lord, thank you for that special moment. Lord, thank you for that idea. Lord, thank you for making me a servant. Lord, thank you for helping me to help others." If you do this, you are going to come into more of God's goodness (and thus, your own goodness) through your **GIVE A DAMN** actions. His blessings are going to come to you more than ever before. God will help you open up doors. He will help turn negative situations around. **GIVE A DAMN** people get ready, because something good is coming your way! You're going to fulfill your God-given destiny because He never forsakes those who **GIVE A DAMN**!

CHAPTER 9

GIVE A DAMN: Actions and Reactions

For every action you take, there is going to be a reaction or response of some kind. How can you react to someone in a positive way? **GIVE A DAMN** people react in a positive but also in a giving way. Yet, they don't think they will get something out of what they give. But ironically, giving and reacting in a positive way will naturally lead to something that will benefit you, without you even expecting it. It will always come back to you in some way.

An issue with a lot of people today is that they feel they have to control everything. Control means you have to win, no matter the cost, in order to fulfill your interests or boost your ego. A **GIVE A DAMN** person is in control when he (or she) helps the other person *feel like he's* in control. This is how you turn control into something positive for both parties. Let me explain. Let's say you look at someone innocently and he responds with a snide, "What are *you* looking at?" A normal reaction might be to say, "What's the matter with you?" or exhibit a non-verbal but equally negative reaction such as an eye roll. By reacting this way, you immediately put the aggressor on the defensive, which generally triggers a more caustic reaction, such as him snapping back something along the lines of, "You've got a problem with me?" This person obviously feels insecure and if you react as though you do have a problem with him, the next thing you know, all hell breaks loose and a fight potentially erupts.

Let's back up and approach this situation differently. The first thing to realize is that something happened to set this person off because of the way you looked at him; it could have been anything, you just don't know. But you *do* know that something is obviously wrong. So now you take responsibility for how you "looked" at this person even though you know you did nothing wrong. My way of approaching this kind of situation is to first find a way to compliment the person, while apologizing at the same time. A method you can use is to focus on a feature of the person's appearance that stands out to you, such as a tattoo, hairstyle, or outfit. After the person says, "What are you looking at?" you could respond, "I'm sorry, I was thinking about how it might be to have a tattoo. Yours looks really well done and I couldn't help but notice it. Please forgive me," or "That hairstyle looks really cool and I was just admiring it, I'm sorry if I appeared to be staring." You get it? Find something to compliment and then apologize. Of course, your words should always be sincere, because if you come across as sarcastic, that makes things even worse. By reacting calmly, and refraining from being aggressive or the aggressor, you take control of the situation, prevent it from getting out of control, and probably make someone feel good at the same time. How many people actually do this? Not many, because they just haven't been educated on dealing with potentially uncomfortable situations, or worse yet, their ego convinces them that the only way to "win" is to react aggressively. Then it's over. The way in which you communicate to people is so vital in controlling every situation.

There is really never a reason to physically fight someone. I am not talking about going to war or defending yourself in a dangerous situation, because that is a whole different ballgame. I am talking about the fights people get into over trivial reasons, usually because they are pushed along by their egos or by jealously. The only reason people fight is because they have to win or prove a point. It's this competitive, must "win at all costs" attitude that creates a problem. Life is not a zero sum game. When you **GIVE A DAMN** you try to relate to what the other person is saying or feeling. Who wants to get hurt anyway? I have never been in a fight. I always try to look at the dynamics of what is going on and understand them before I react. I attempt to relate to the other person and understand *why* he is acting in such a way. Does that make me weak or wimpy? Nope. No one wins when a fight erupts. I know how to control a situation by trying to understand it and keeping my emotions in check. The best way to avoid a fight is to apologize and compliment. It works every time. When you compliment in a highly charged situation, it builds the other person's sense of self worth, even if it's just for a short instant. When someone tries to provoke a fight, they are ultimately looking for a boost to their self confidence, it makes them feel big! You make a person believe that he has won the battle, but you have really won by controlling the situation. This does, however, take quick thinking.

For example, let's say you walk by a guy with a beautiful woman, and you stare at her longer than you should (this has actually happened to me). The guy turns to you abruptly, and says, "What are you looking at her like that for?" You should never say, "I wasn't looking at her," (especially with a look of disgust on your face) because you have suggested to him indirectly that he is an idiot for thinking that way. Your behavior tells him that his suspicion is right and that he did catch you looking at his girlfriend. This feeds even more anger and a fight could erupt. My response would be, "I am sorry, is this your girlfriend?" you ask. He says, "YES!" Now you say (which is true), "I was just admiring your girlfriend and I just wish one day that I could find one as pretty. You must feel very lucky, and please forgive me; I did not mean anything by it." What can he say now? In every potential difficult situation you should apologize and compliment. And by doing so, any potential conflict will be defused. You **GIVE A DAMN**, you don't want anyone to get hurt and you make people feel good about something. Compliment all of the time. It goes a long, long way and people remember it.

Some will say that people who **GIVE A DAMN** can usually be taken advantage of by those who don't. For example, when I was running the non-profit Louisiana Technology Council (LTC), we helped open up a Business Recovery Center after Hurricane Katrina that provided free phone, Internet, office furniture and a computer to those businesses that were affected by the storm; all for a small fee of $150 a month. However, there was one tenant who decided he wasn't going to pay, and he did not pay for several months. All along he was making promises (and we believed him) but never paid. For months we tried to recover what he owed us without success so we attempted to evict him. He then sued us because according to the law, we could not evict anyone without going through a time consuming and costly procedure. As we got closer to trial, he disappeared. The LTC wound up losing six months of rent and paying thousands of dollars in legal fees. He took advantage of us. He didn't **GIVE A DAMN** about what the LTC did to help him through his loss. He only cared about taking advantage of the LTC, and used the legal system to his advantage. Unfortunately, these types of occurrences happen frequently and it's part of life. Yet, these situations should not deter anyone from maintaining a **GIVE A DAMN** attitude. After all, even if you don't benefit from one instance, you will be rewarded in countless others.

This being said, **GIVE A DAMN** people cannot continue to **GIVE A DAMN** about others if these same people don't eventually **GIVE A DAMN** in return. I have already mentioned that you should never expect anything in return when you **GIVE A DAMN**, but not to the point of being taken advantage of. **GIVE A DAMN** people will shy away from others who continue to be self-centered, negative, hurtful, or entitled. Sometimes we know who these people are and it is not hard to single them out. By identifying and avoiding these people, we can concentrate our own **GIVE A DAMN** attitudes on those who **GIVE A DAMN** about us as well. Can non **GIVE A DAMN** people be changed? I really hope so but and it will take a collective effort by all of us.

Sports Contracts Gone Haywire

For two seasons, former New Orleans Saints running back, Deuce McAllister, suffered from torn ligaments to both knees. He rehabbed one knee the first time after tearing it in the middle of the season. Upon his return, he tore the ligament in his other knee and had to go through the same rigorous treatment. Before the second knee was rehabbed, Deuce was supposed to get a $1 million dollar roster signing bonus. He could have demanded this signing bonus even though he still had not fully recovered from his second knee problem; instead he agreed to defer the roster bonus until such time that he could see if he could play again. He could have demanded the bonus, but didn't. Why would he do this? Because he is not a greedy or self centered person. How many times have you ever heard of such an act being done in pro sports? Probably never. He thought about the team and their interest before he thought of himself.

I get tired of professional athletes making zillions of dollars and then complaining that it's not enough after having a good season; so they want their multi-year contract re-negotiated. It's just wrong. What happens if they have a bad season? Do they go to the management and say, "I want to re-negotiate my contract to a lower salary because I did not do very well last season?" Of course not. And have you ever heard management asking a player to do the same thing (take a lesser salary in the middle of a contract) because they played badly the previous year? A player makes a commitment to a contract because he feels that at the time it was fair or a good deal. If we agree to something, we should honor that commitment regardless of the circumstances that might come later.

This brings up another example of a player in my own backyard who I have a lot of respect for, Drew Brees, quarterback for the New Orleans Saints. Although he is a great player, my admiration for him stems from his conduct off the field, not on it. When his contract ran out in 2011, he stated that he would be "beyond stunned" if he and the Saints were unable to agree on a contract extension, echoing the same comments by his coach. Brees stated that he did not believe his next deal would prevent the Saints from bidding on other key members of their record-setting offense who were to become free agents. "My number one priority, and it always has been this, is keeping our team together and making sure we have the right guys in the right positions to make a run at this for a long time," Brees told the Associated Press. "We all kind of work together on this thing. Put it this way: I'm not worried one bit about my contract or our ability to keep guys at key positions." And yet Brees was expected to command an annual salary in the range of $18 million, which would be commensurate with the average yearly pay of top quarterbacks in the league such as Tom Brady and Peyton Manning.

Drew is what this book is all about. He is a consummate individual who truly **GIVES A DAMN**. If more people adopted an attitude like Drew Brees, this world would be a much better place. Thank you, Drew Brees, for setting this positive example. And you know what else? Brees had previously signed a 5-year deal with the Saints, which had one of the most potent offenses in the NFL. Brees set numerous records during those 5 years, but did he ever demand a re-negotiation of his contract because he did so well? Not a chance. But others have done it in sports. They have a great year and want to renegotiate their contract because now they feel they did not get a fair deal and even threaten to sit out a year if they don't. Very sad.

GIVE A DAMN people put the goals of the team before their own. A lot of people have individual goals but when you sacrifice a team goal for an individual goal, you are thinking like a self centered person. Let me bring up another example concerning the New Orleans Saints football team. All you heard from Saints players was how they could win a championship. The camaraderie in the locker room focused on the team. You *never* heard one complaint, criticism or condemnation from any player. They did not brag but simply went out and did their job for the team. However, all it takes is one individual to outwardly act in a self centered way and then it begins to have a cancerous effect on the team. The problem with many good teams is that they think individually and never become a great "team." And it evolves around character. Character to **GIVE A DAMN**. Character to think of others and what is good for the team. Character to motivate people even if you are not the star player or second string. Character is the difference maker when it comes to championship teams. *Everyone* on a team that **GIVES A DAMN** becomes a champion.

I'll bet most of you can think of hundreds of ways you did not **GIVE A DAMN** at certain points in your life, and it was probably because you were not aware of what you might have done. Some people know how to **GIVE A DAMN** because this type of attitude was nurtured from a young age (meaning Mom and Dad taught you well). It became instinctive because it was learned. These people just naturally think of others. How can you learn to be a **GIVE A DAMN** person? It's about awareness, attitude, practice, and a desire to make it happen. It really focuses on one's attitude. Earl Nightingale said it best: "We become what we think about." You will return to what is planted in your brain over and over again. Plant in your brain the simple phrase, "**GIVE A DAMN**," and you will become that person. Write the phrase, **GIVE A DAMN** on file cards as a constant reminder, and put them everywhere that you will see them. They say it takes twenty-one days to learn a new habit. What is really gratifying is this: when you do **GIVE A DAMN** you will begin to feel a great sense of satisfaction. Don't be discouraged by those around you who don't **GIVE A DAMN**. Just trust how important this is for a better society. We need to do this one person at a time, and more importantly we need to have a much greater focus on teaching the **GIVE A DAMN** attitude in our school systems.

I think it is so important to change our beliefs and attitudes and learn to **GIVE A DAMN**. It begins in the classroom, at home and in our own minds. It begins with knowing what is right and what is wrong and with making the right choices. Changing a culture will take a long time but we have to start with our kids and stamp it into their psyche by teaching and modeling a **GIVE A DAMN** attitude early on. We have to start now if we want change, and we need to teach adults and children at the same time. Adults need it as much as kids, and the younger the kids are when they learn it, the easier it will be for them to implement it throughout their lives.

Learning to **GIVE A DAMN** will not be easy. The best way to **GIVE A DAMN** is to continually ask yourself this question, "How can I **GIVE A DAMN**?" Each time you will get the right answer. You just have to listen. Don't try to justify behaviors in your mind when you know they are wrong. Pay attention and listen to the voice in your mind that is telling you the right thing to do, and don't ignore it.

Here are some simple things you can do to show that you **GIVE A DAMN**:

- Put the dishes in the dishwasher when you are finished
- Scoop up your dog's droppings, rather than leaving the mess for someone else
- Hurry across the street when a car stops for you
- If you are in a grocery checkout lane and have a full basket, let someone go ahead of you when he or she only has a few items

- Say, "Thank You," *whenever* someone does or says something nice
- Say, "Excuse me," when you impede someone's way
- Say, "Please," whenever you request something whether verbal or written
- Compliment or show appreciation all the time
- Hold the door or elevator open for someone, regardless of gender and even if they are several steps away, wait for them
- Don't throw trash out of your car (you would not throw it on the floor of your own residence would you?)
- When you use a cart after shopping put it in the location reserved for carts or bring it back to the entrance
- Don't throw your cigarette butt out of the car
- If you hit (or even bump) an unoccupied car and it causes a dent or scratch of some kind, don't run off! Leave a note with your number on it
- If a cashier gives you more in change than you deserve, give it back
- When driving, stay in the right lane unless you are passing
- Pick up trash on the ground and throw it away
- Return a phone call when someone you know has left you a message
- Return an email from someone you know who takes the time to reach out to you personally
- Wave your hand as a gesture of thanks when someone lets you into traffic
- Men, put the toilet seat up before doing your business (and then put it down again for the next person)
- Clean up the grass clippings when cutting grass and don't blow them in the street for someone else to clean up.
- If you pick up a folded piece of clothing at a retail store, fold it and put back it like you found it
- Think about spending other people's money (even corporate money) like it is your own

- If you drive a car that has a disability sticker or license plate and you or your passengers are not disabled, don't park in the handicapped spot just because you can

You and I could probably list hundreds of more examples that show how to **GIVE A DAMN**. Just take the initiative and do it.

CHAPTER 10

Conclusion

There was a 46 year-old professor from Carnegie Mellon named Randy Pausch. He gave one final lecture to his students because he had terminal cancer. He had fought it, beaten it, and then it came back. Randy was always a dreamer, dreaming about what could be done and how he could go about doing it. He always had challenges, yet he always kept going. I was very inspired by this speech because he was such a positive person. I listened to his last speech before he died and several things struck me. First, I knew that he would really relate to this book. He talked about how important it was to show gratitude, how to apologize and to have the Disney "Tigger" attitude, that is, to maintain a smile and a positive mood at all times. What hit me the most was how he emphasized the importance of people over things. He said there are three things people should always do if they make a mistake: 1) Say I'm sorry (compassion); 2) Admit that it was your fault (take responsibility for what you do); and 3) Ask the question, "How do I make it right?" (taking responsibility for fixing the mistake, no matter how painful it is).

I have *hope* and I firmly believe that **GIVE A DAMN** is already built into everyone's psyche. It just needs to be brought out. When there is a catastrophic event in nature, it is truly remarkable how people **GIVE A DAMN** to help others. They come out in droves to help without expecting anything in return. There is this pervasive attitude to help others because of what happened. Why is it that when something major happens to people, we truly want to help those in need? Do we feel guilty? Do we feel an obligation? Do we feel sorry for them? Why can't people **GIVE A DAMN** all of the time like that? It seems that the more dire the situation, the more people **GIVE A DAMN**. This gives me hope that most people truly do **GIVE A DAMN**. They just don't know how to do it all of the time because they have not learned it as part of their psyche. It takes a major and visible event to bring it out.

All little children are, for the most part, very humble, honest, and sincere. You see it all the time. So why can't we become more like children? I do not mean childlike, but rather of a pure heart. A child starts out being innocent of the evils of the world, and is naturally trusting. Children generally trust whatever an adult tells them and they have no preconceived ideas in their mind; they are excited to learn all they can with honest curiosity. Since they are very impressionable at an early age, they can be easily taught how to **GIVE A DAMN**, (actually in their case it should be called **GIVE A DARN**) and yet they are not. Next time you see a 3, 4 or 5 year-old, think about what is being taught to them about today's society. We have to change our thinking in order to change the thinking of our future. The kids are it. When we apply "the child" to ourselves, it means that we must be humble, honest and have a giving heart. We must also have the desire to learn with an open mind, just like children do.

You determine your attitude when you **GIVE A DAMN**. No one else will do it for you, although your actions can have a profound effect on someone else. You have to have a certain mindset to make it happen. As I have suggested earlier, you might want to carry a card around in your wallet or in your handbag that reminds you to **GIVE A DAMN**; have a card on your desk, in your car, or anywhere that will provide you with a visible reminder as to what it means. Better yet, buy the wristband that says: "**GIVE A DAMN**," which can be your permanent reminder wherever you go; and make sure you show others. The **GIVE A DAMN** attitude is tied to a willingness to be responsible and make it happen. It starts with you. Just think if you saw someone else wearing the same **GIVE A DAMN** wristband as you; and that there were millions of people doing the same thing. How would you feel? I know that I would feel terrific because I was perhaps making a difference in today's society, and someone is with me doing the same thing!

Think about what it would be like to be in someone else's shoes. Wouldn't you want him to be honest with you? Wouldn't you want him to admit to you when he made a mistake? Wouldn't you want him to make it right? Wouldn't you want him to apologize? Wouldn't you want him to take responsibility for his actions? Of course you would. Yet there are many times we don't think this way when the shoe is on the other foot. I catch myself sometimes because I want to justify what I did was right by offering an excuse. This kind of behavior is becoming an epidemic in today's society. We have to change our thinking.

Think about it this way. If you are comfortable and are *willing to go public* with any of your actions (meaning on any decision that you make or any action that you take), then it is a sure bet that you are doing the right thing. You are not keeping anything "hidden" so to speak and you are setting an example for others to follow. So if you are willing to conduct your actions in an *open manner*, then it's a pretty safe bet that you do **GIVE A DAMN**.

COMMITMENT
HONESTY
ACCOUNTABILITY
RESPECT
COURAGE
ETHICS
INTEGRITY

These are words that we need to live by. **GIVE A DAMN** encompasses all of these words and then some. But these are nothing more than words unless we actually live by them. Our greatest challenge is to behave according to our beliefs and one of these beliefs should be to **GIVE A DAMN**. We must practice it on a daily basis. We must make it our attitude and live by it totally. So what does it take to **GIVE A DAMN**?

> **Commitment** – Means to fight the temptation to compromise the values that the words **GIVE A DAMN** encompass
> **Honesty** – Means telling the truth, regardless of its consequences
> **Accountability** – Means holding ourselves to high standards, and taking responsibility when we fall short of these standards
> **Respect** – Means we need to treat others with dignity, no matter who they are
> **Courage** – Means having the wherewithal to maintain a **GIVE A DAMN** attitude even in tough circumstances and to follow your conscience instead of following the crowd
> **Ethics** – Means adhering to the right conduct, even though doing or trying to justify the wrong conduct might be convenient or easy
> **Integrity** – Means you maintain consistent moral principles, and feel a sense of pride in your Mom's (or God's) eyes and your own.

Internalizing these seven values will turn you into a person of true quality. We all have an inner voice guiding us towards these principles; there's just a tremendous amount of noise that we have to filter out in order to hear it. We have to listen. **GIVE A DAMN** matters. It is the only thing that can make this world better. I firmly believe this and my hope is that you agree also.

It will take years for the **GIVE A DAMN** revolution to get in gear and for people to shift to a **GIVE A DAMN** focus and attitude. Many years ago our world used to embrace this conscience thinking a lot more than we do today. Our society has deteriorated over the past several years because of our self-serving attitude. My goal is for this book to guide you and others towards a better mindset. We *can* make a difference, one person at a time. So, we have a choice, and we should choose to start each day by saying, "I **GIVE A DAMN**," and make this part of our daily routine. If you do this, you will be amazed at how good you will feel over the long term.

Commitment to GIVE A DAMN

Be Truthful. Lying is often a gut-level defensive reaction to a perceived danger. When you feel the desire to hide the truth, take the time to jot down what you will get out of a trusting relationship versus the short-term gain you might get out of evading the truth.

Think *before* **You Act!** Review the ethics of planned decisions or activities before implementing them. Use the questions below (or similar ones) as your litmus test. Answering "no" to one or more of the following questions would suggest a need for you to change your thinking and if you cannot, maybe you might need to seek counsel or advice from appropriate sources (or read this book over and over again ☺):

- Is it legal?
- Does it comply with appropriate rules and guidelines?
- Is it in sync with my personal or organizational values that relate to others?
- Will I honestly be comfortable and guilt-free if I do it?
- Does it match my stated commitment to doing the right thing and making the right decisions?
- Would I do it to my family or friends?
- Would my mother approve?
- Would I be perfectly okay with someone doing it to me?
- Would the most ethical person I know do it?

Create something that people just cannot walk away from. Create an "environmental" attitude that people want to be around. This will then influence and inspire them to become a **GIVE A DAMN** person just like you. A **GIVE A DAMN** attitude is contagious!

Final Comments

The author and clergyman Charles R. Swindoll once wrote a paragraph on attitude that I will cite here in full because of how much it applies to the topic of this book. He said:

"The longer I live, the more I realize the impact of attitude on life. Attitude, to me, is more important than facts. It is more important than the past, than education, than money, than circumstances, than failures, than successes, than what other people think or say or do. It is more important than appearance, giftedness, or skill. It will make or break a company ... a church ... a home. The remarkable thing is we have a choice every day regarding the attitude we will embrace for that day. We cannot change our past. We cannot change the fact that people will act in a certain way. We cannot change the inevitable. The only thing we can do is play on the one string we have: Attitude... I am convinced that life is 10% what happens to me, and 90% how I react to it."

And so it is with you ... we are in charge of our attitude or how we **GIVE A DAMN**!

One hundred years from now, it will not matter how much money you had or made, the house you lived in, or the kind of car you drove. I can give you all the guidelines, rules, and principles you need to **GIVE A DAMN**, but frankly these are just words, words to live by; but until you actually use them to shape your actions, you can't call yourself a **GIVE A DAMN** person. But the world may be different because you, as a **GIVE A DAMN** person, were important in the life of not just one person but all the people whose lives you touch. Yet even these people will not be on this earth forever. But in the end, your maker (and Mom) will know how many people you touched and how much you did to **GIVE A DAMN**. **GIVE A DAMN** is a choice. It is the result of sincere intention, diligent effort, intelligent direction and skillful execution. It also requires a humble (but not submissive) manner of carrying yourself through the world. It is not something you are obligated to give, but something you do anyway, not for yourself but for others. **GIVE A DAMN** represents a wise choice among many alternatives. Let's hope you make the right choice.

By reading this book to the end, I believe you are committed to being a **GIVE A DAMN** person. Throughout this book I have emphasized many of the same points in a variety of ways. I have done this on purpose to drive home my passion on what it means to **GIVE A DAMN**. I have learned throughout my life that the more you read and hear something, the more it becomes part of you. Hopefully **GIVE A DAMN** becomes a major part of who you are.

I hope you will go to our Facebook page and our web site at www.**GIVEADAMN**book.com and sign your name on as one who truly does **GIVES A DAMN**. Most important, purchase our **GIVE A DAMN** wristband(s), wear it and then hand them out to everyone you know. Tell people about this book. Our goal is to do this one person at a time until we reach 1 million **GIVE A DAMN** people, then 2 million, then 3 million, and until the entire world knows how to **GIVE A DAMN**. Is this a challenge? Yes, however, when you **GIVE A DAMN**, anything is possible.

**"Individually we make a difference,
collectively we change the world!"**

Good luck and may God Bless you always.

PS I started with this comment and I am going to end with this comment. You might feel **GIVE A DAMN** is a harsh statement, and if you do, I respectfully disagree. However, I understand how some could be offended by this slogan so I will ask you once again to change all the **GIVE A DAMN** statements that you have read in this book to **SHARE YOUR LOVE,** and you will accomplish the same objectives. Join me as we do both. Most of all, thank you for reading this book.

Made in the USA
Charleston, SC
22 January 2017